Willa Cather

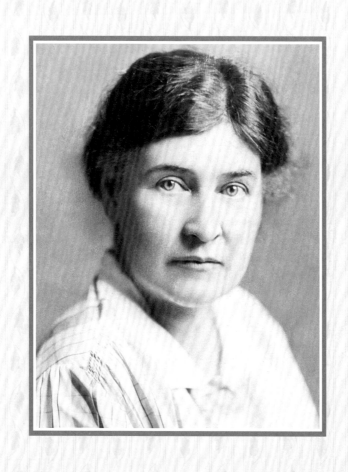

A BIOGRAPHY

Willa Cather

MILTON MELTZER

Twenty-First Century Books
Minneapolis

Cover photo of Willa Cather used with permission of Willa Cather Archives & Special Collections, University of Nebraska-Lincoln Libraries. Background photo used with permission of © Panoramic Images/Getty Images.

The images in this book are used with permission of: © Hulton Archive/Getty Images, p. 2; Willa Cather Archives & Special Collections, University of Nebraska-Lincoln Libraries , pp. 11, 12 (both), 13, 14 (both), 16, 23, 29, 33 (both), 36, 38, 44, 45 (both), 55, 58, 59, 60, 61, 63, 67, 74, 78, 82, 87, 93 (both), 94, 99, 105, 108, 109, 111, 113 (both), 115, 116, 125, 126, 131, 142; Nebraska State Historical Society, pp. 20, 21, 24, 27 (both), 30, 31, 35, 39, 40, 42 (both), 47 (both), 56, 118, 137; © Bettmann/CORBIS, pp. 43, 70, 107, 121 (top), 133; Library of Congress, pp. 49 (LC-D4-33486), 68 (LC-DIG-ggbain-05453), 83 (LC-USZ62-82912), 89 (LC-USZ62-89479), 102 (LC-USZ62-82911), 121 (bottom) (LC-USZ62-82914); Humanities and Social Sciences Library/Photography Collection Miriam and Ira D. Wallach Division of Art, Prints and Photographs, The New York Public Library, Astor, Lenox and Tilden Foundations, pp. 51, 73; Humanities and Social Sciences Library/general research division, The New York Public Library, Astor, Lenox and Tilden Foundations, p. 140.

Twenty-First Century Books
A division of Lerner Publishing Group, Inc.
241 First Avenue North
Minneapolis, MN 55401 U.S.A.

Website address: www.lernerbooks.com

Library of Congress Cataloging-in-Publication Data

Meltzer, Milton, 1915–
Willa Cather : a biography / by Milton Meltzer.
    p.   cm. — (Literary greats)
Includes bibliographical references (p. 150) and index.
ISBN 978-0-8225-7604-4 (alk. paper)
1. Cather, Willa, 1873–1947—Juvenile literature. 2. Novelists, American—
20th century—Biography—Juvenile literature. I. Title.
PS3505.A87Z7423 2008   813'.52—dc22 [B]   2007025629

Manufactured in the United States of America
1 2 3 4 5 6 – BP – 13 12 11 10 09 08

Also by Milton Meltzer

Carl Sandburg: A Biography

Case Closed: The Real Scoop on Detective Work

Edgar Allan Poe: A Biography

Emily Dickinson: A Biography

*Hear That Train Whistle Blow! How the Railroad
Changed the World*

Henry David Thoreau: A Biography

Herman Melville: A Biography

Hour of Freedom: American History in Poetry

Langston Hughes: A Biography

Nathaniel Hawthorne: A Biography

Pizarro and the Conquest of Peru

Ten Kings and the Worlds They Ruled

Ten Queens: Portraits of Women of Power

The Day the Sky Fell: A History of Terrorism

There Comes a Time: The Struggle for Civil Rights

They Came in Chains: The Story of the Slave Ships

Tough Times (a novel)

Walt Whitman: A Biography

Witches and Witch-Hunts: A History of Persecution

Contents

Introduction

Readers who enter the world of Willa Cather's fiction for the first time may wish to start with her best novel. But when they seek the opinion of scholars and critics, they find one says *My Ántonia* is her finest work; another calls *Death Comes for the Archbishop* the best; and still another will say *Shadows on the Rock*—that's the one!

Where does that leave the beginner? Where he or she should be—eager to read all these and more. Willa Cather created twelve novels and many more short stories. Almost all of them are still in print. They are a treasure no one should miss exploring.

And that is true of Willa Cather's life. Her rich talent was developed by life in so many different places. In Virginia soon after the Civil War (1861–1865). In Nebraska when pioneers were struggling to make a living on the barren prairie. In steel town Pittsburgh, in metropolitan New York, in Boston, Canada, London, Paris, Rome . . . .

"If a true artist were born in a pigpen and raised in a sty," she once said, "he would still find inspiration for this work. Everywhere is a storehouse of literary material. The only need is the eye to see."

CHAPTER ONE
Willie
of Virginia

WILLA CATHER WAS RAISED in nothing like a pigpen. She was born on December 7, 1873, in the Back Creek Valley of Virginia, about 13 miles (16 kilometers) west of the town of Winchester. Several generations back, the first Cather to emigrate left Wales and settled in the Virginia Colony. His great grandson, Charles Cather, married Mary Virginia Boak in 1872.

Willa, the first of their seven children, was born a year later. The infant was named Wilella, after a young aunt who had recently died. Until she reached her teens, everyone called her Willie, a name she liked. Finally, she modified it to Willa.

The young parents were a handsome couple, though quite different in personality. Charles was an easygoing man, but Mary was a hard-driving woman who sometimes rubbed people—including Willa—the wrong way.

Willa's paternal grandfather, William Cather, was opposed to slavery and had remained loyal to the North during the Civil War.

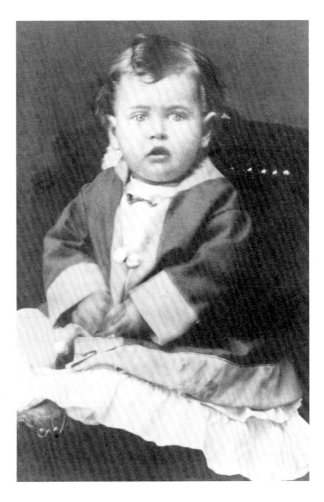

Willa Cather was born in 1873 and baptized as Wilella Love Cather. She would later change her first name to Willa and her middle name to Sibert, her grandmother Boak's maiden name. She would even change her birth year to 1876.

He owned no slaves and had run his farm with the help of hired labor and his sons, George and Charles. (The boys avoided the draft by moving temporarily to West Virginia.) Doing well, William expanded to more than 300 acres (121 hectares) and built an imposing home. His three-story, brick farmhouse was called Willow Shade. It had five bedrooms, each with its own fireplace. Surrounding it were great willow trees, a spacious lawn, and a box hedge running down to a creek. Just beyond was the highway known as the Northwest Turnpike.

Willa Cather's parents: Charles Cather (left), *a deputy sheriff, and Mary Virginia (Jennie) Boak Cather* (right)

Although the Civil War had ended eight years before Willa's birth, the scars of that long and bloody conflict had scarcely healed. Though Willa's paternal grandparents had supported the Union (Northern) cause, three of her mother's brothers had fought for the Confederacy (the South). Passions had been powerful on both sides, and during the stormy Reconstruction period (1863–1877), they continued to flare up.

Somehow Willa's mother succeeded in reuniting the divided family. Later, the adult Willa would shy away from causes, whether political or social, trusting herself and others to do the right thing and to offer generous help to individuals in need.

It was at Willow Shade that Willa lived most of her first nine years. The Cathers' acreage was too rocky for growing crops, so

Willa's father raised sheep for sale at the Baltimore (Maryland) market. In their huge barn was a mill that ground feed for the sheep. With Willow Shade on a main highway, relatives and friends often dropped in, sometimes staying for a day or two or even a month. The Cathers employed both white and black house servants. Everyone took a hand in preparing and serving food, weaving, sewing, spinning, and making candles and quilts.

Willa's grandfather William Cather built Willow Shade, the house where Willa was born and lived for her first nine years. William Cather and his wife, Caroline, are just barely visible on Willow Shade's front porch in this photo from the 1870s.

Early on, Willa became the older sister to two boys, Roscoe and Douglass, and a girl, Jessica. As the family expanded, Willa's maternal grandmother, Rachel Boak, a widow, came to live with them and help. Later, when the family moved to Nebraska, there would be three more children: James, Jack, and Elsie. Many of the people in this large household would one day figure in Willa Cather's fiction.

 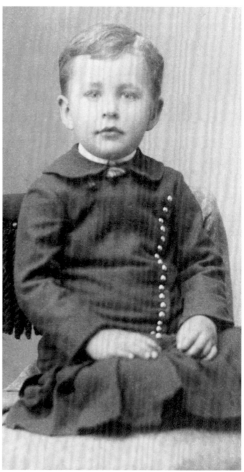

Willa's two closest brothers in age, Roscoe (left) *and Douglass* (right), *pose for portraits in the early 1880s.*

Willa was homeschooled. Grandmother Boak taught her to read and write, and read aloud to her from the Bible, *Pilgrim's Progress*, and *Peter Parley's Universal History*.

The earliest evidence of Willa's writing was found on an almost illegible scrap of paper. In a childish scribble (with her original spelling), she told the world why dogs were better than cats:

> The dog is a very intelligent animal. . . . The nature
> of most dogs is kind, noble and generous. O! how dif-
> ferent from the snarling, spitting crul cat. . . . New
> foundland dogs are also famous for their way of saving
> the lives of people when drowning. And the St. Bren-
> ards are often trained in Switzerland to find travelers
> in the snow and carry them to a place of safety.
> Pugs & Poodles are famous for nothing unless it is their
> expensive funerals which sometimes amont to one
> thousand dollars. Lord Byron, one of our greatest poets
> wrote a beautiful elegy on a dog, who ever wrote eny-
> thing on a Cat? Did you ever see a tall massive dog
> with curly hair bright eyes and a knowing air? Did you
> ever see a poor thin scraggy cat, with dirty hair dull
> green eyes and drooping tail. If so I leave it to your
> common sense to answer for I know you will say the
> noble majestic dog.

With a wide world just beyond the front door, Willa roved the woods and streams, fishing, trapping animals, and studying the birds and insects. She often stayed much of the day in the fields to help her father herd the sheep. At evening, when he drove the sheep into the fold, he would carry Willa on his shoulders. She loved the big farmhouse and "every tree and every rock, every landmark of the countryside, all the familiar faces, all their things . . . all their ways."

Willa poses for a photograph in the late 1870s. Willa was extra-ordinarily impressionable at this young age and was later able to vividly recall events from her early childhood for use in her novels.

When Willa was five years old, she witnessed a family event she'd never forget. It happened at Willow Shade on a March evening in 1879. Willa, nursing a cold, was in her mother's room on the third floor, propped up high on two pillows. Through the window, she could watch the turnpike and spy the coming of the stagecoach her mother and Old Till, their black servant, were waiting for. She'd been told that Nancy Till, who'd been a slave in Grandma Boak's household, would be arriving any minute, all the way from Canada. She had lived there as a free woman ever since that time twenty-five years earlier when Grandma's daughter Rachel Boak had helped her run away to freedom on the Underground Railroad.

Suddenly Willa's mother ran into the room, pulled the blanket close around Willa, and carried her to the window. Looking out, she saw the coach's horses come to a halt before the front door. A woman in a black coat and a turban stepped down and entered the house. A few minutes later, the bedroom door opened, and in came Nancy Till, a tall, gold-skinned woman, embraced by her mother, Old Till, whom she had not seen in so many years.

Sixty years later, Willa would use this event in her last novel.

George Cather, one of Willa's uncles, had earlier moved to the frontier territory of Nebraska. In 1874 Willa's grandparents went west to spend the winter with George, who was their son. They believed the humid climate of their section of Virginia was to blame for the tuberculosis that had sickened many members of the family and killed several. (Later, in 1882, scientist Robert Koch would demonstrate that the disease was an infection caused by the tubercle bacillus. Not until the 1950s would antibiotics be developed to treat the disease.) Grandpa Cather himself was not well and felt the drier climate of the western plains would provide a healthier place for him as well as a good environment for raising a family.

Together with other Virginians, Grandpa made plans to settle in the West. They chose a broad plateau of land between two rivers in Nebraska, called the Divide. Soon after these pioneers had established homes on the prairie, Willa's father decided to join his parents and his brother. He sold Willow Shade in 1883 and moved the whole family to Nebraska.

For Willa, as for any child who'd known such joys in the earliest years, leaving home was heartbreaking. In her mind, she would always remain a southerner. Later, she dipped into these early memories to write some of her first short stories. But she never treated southern life in a novel until the very last one she wrote.

CHAPTER TWO

What Will the Neighbors Think?

WHAT WAS NEBRASKA LIKE when Willa's family settled there? The territory had entered the Union only sixteen years prior to their arrival. Long before, when Spanish and French explorers and the fur traders had come, the land was occupied by several Native American tribes. The United States took possession of the territory through the Louisiana Purchase of 1803. Not until 1823 did immigrants establish their first permanent settlement. And soon, after deadly clashes, the Native Americans were forced to move to reservations.

Nebraska! What a contrast with Virginia. The flat windswept prairie of the one and the hill-and-dale landscape of the other. And the sheer immensity—Nebraska was well over twice the size of Virginia. The name *Nebraska* comes from an Indian word meaning "flat water." Later, when Nebraska became a leader in agriculture, it was nicknamed the Cornhusker State.

Willa's family arrived by train after an endless journey across the prairie of the region. To the nine-year-old, the countryside

The Nebraska prairie that Willa saw as she traveled across the state in 1883 can still be seen in modern times. Land near Red Cloud, Nebraska, was acquired in 2006 to be the Willa Cather Memorial Prairie. Members of the Willa Cather Foundation are working to return the nearly 600 acres (243 hectares) to its native grasslands.

looked as bare as a sheet of metal. Her grandfather met them at the station with his horse and wagon and carried them to his farm. It was located in Webster County, about halfway across the southern part of the state. Many years later, Willa recalled that day, describing it to an interviewer:

We drove out from Red Cloud to my grandfather's homestead one day in April. I was sitting on the hay in the bottom of a Studebaker wagon, holding on to the side of the wagon box to steady myself—the roads were mostly faint trails over the bunch grass in those days. The land was open range and there was almost no fencing. As we drove further and further out into the country, I felt a good deal as if we had come to the end of everything—it was a kind of erasure of personality. . . . I had heard my father say you had to show grit in a new country, and I would have got on pretty well during the ride if it had not been for the larks. Every now and then one flew up and sang a few splendid notes and dropped down in the grass again. That reminded me of something—I don't know what, but my one purpose in life just then was not to cry, and every time they did it, I thought I would go under.

Willa lived on a farmstead similar to this one during her first years in Nebraska. This house is part of the George Cather Farmstead, located near Red Cloud. Willa's uncle and aunt, George and Francis Cather, lived here. Willa later used it as the setting in her 1922 novel, One of Ours.

That mood of despair did not persist. Willa gradually came to enjoy life on the farm. For a time, however, she experienced some kind of illness that paralyzed her to the point that she had to rely on a crutch to move about. But she had a pony, and she rode it to a postal station (called Catherton) a few miles off to pick up mail and distribute it to neighbors in their sod farm-houses on her way back. Often she'd stop to visit a bit and exchange gossip and news, gathering impressions of folks she'd never known before. They were uprooted too but from far more distant—and different—places. She came to feel an emotional bond with these Germans, Poles, Russians, Bohemians, Swedes, and Danes. Many of them would turn up later in Willa Cather's stories.

It was the Homestead Act of 1862 and the coming of the railroads that opened up this vast region of the West for settlement. It offered citizens or future citizens over the age of twenty-one a grant of 160 acres (65 hectares) of public land if they lived on the property for five years, improved it, and paid a small registration fee. If a family was willing to pay $1.25 an acre, they could obtain the land after only six months' residence.

Still, Nebraska would never boast a large population. When the year 2000 opened a new century, the state still had fewer than two million people. But it managed to raise a number of distinguished people: actors Harold Lloyd, Henry Fonda, and Marlon Brando; dancer Fred Astaire; presidential candidate William Jennings Bryan; and the Oglala Sioux Chief, Red Cloud; and, of course, Willa Cather.

Willa soon learned that most Americans, including her own family, were not much interested in "foreigners." Long after she'd left to live in the East, she said: "Our settlers . . . cautious and convinced of their own superiority, kept themselves isolated as much as possible from foreign influences." But if one of them were sick or in trouble, kind neighbors would lend a hand.

The Cathers moved to this house in Red Cloud in 1884. Willa would live in this house until she went off to college in 1890. Her family lived here until they moved to another house in Red Cloud in 1904.

Men and women from almost all corners of Europe, it seemed, were laboring to create cornfields on a prairie where only wild, rough red grass had been growing for eons. About a year after they arrived, Willa's father decided he'd had it. He held on to the acreage he'd acquired and would continue to add to it. But he decided to make better use of his talents in the nearby town of Red Cloud. As a young man, he'd studied law in Baltimore for two years. He opened an office and dealt with farm loans and mortgages. His clients noted that he kept his Virginia accent and his southern manners.

And Red Cloud—what was it like? It was named, ironically, for the Sioux chief of that region whose people had been displaced from land guaranteed to them by the U.S. government. When the Cathers moved into their rented house there, about

The original two-story section of the railroad depot in Red Cloud (shown here in 1910) was built in 1897. With eight passenger trains running through the depot daily, it was a busy place when Cather lived in Red Cloud.

twenty-five hundred people lived in this county seat, which was clustered around the railroad depot. The Chicago, Burlington and Quincy Railroad, known simply as the Burlington, branched out in all directions, including south into Kansas. Eight trains came through daily, and a hotel and restaurant catered to the needs of the passengers.

Moving to Red Cloud for Willa was yet another displacement—but this time, not so unhappy. Her schooling up to then had been in Grandmother Boak's hands and then a few months in a little one-room school near Catherton. In the Red Cloud classrooms, she met a mix of pupils she found very interesting. Foremost among them was Annie Sadilek (later known as Annie Pavelka), a Bohemian girl who would years later become the title character in *My Ántonia*.

Among her teachers were several she admired and with whom she remained in touch long after.

One of these teachers was Evangeline King. Willa recalled that "Miss King was the first person whom I cared a great deal for outside of my own family. I had been in her class only a few weeks when I wanted more than anything else in the world to please her." When Willa moved up to high school, Miss King continued to help her, especially with algebra, a subject Willa felt she'd never master.

Willa had the kind of mind that kept probing, seeking, and questioning. She reached out to anyone in the town who seemed to promise something new and enlightening. This led her to Mr. and Mrs. Charles Wiener, Jewish immigrants who ran a store and spoke German and French. They opened their well-stocked private library to Willa. She began to read French and hoped to go on to German. From their frequent conversations, she learned something about life where the Wieners came from (he from Germany and she from France) and believed that one day she'd see Europe for herself.

In her story "Old Mrs. Harris," Cather offers a portrait of herself as a teenager (Vickie) visiting Mrs. Wiener (Mrs. Rosen):

> She wasn't pretty, yet Mrs. Rosen found her attractive. She liked her sturdy build, and the steady vitality that glowed in her rosy skin and dark blue eyes—even gave a springy quality to her curly reddish-brown hair, which she still wore in a single braid down her back. Mrs. Rosen liked to have Vickie about because she was never listless or dreamy or apathetic. A half-smile nearly always played about her lips and eyes, and it was there because she was pleased with something, not because she wanted to be agreeable. Even a half-smile made her cheeks dimple. She had what her mother called 'a happy disposition.'

There were others in Red Cloud who sensed how remarkable was this young girl's mind. Among them was a German piano teacher, Professor Schindelmeisser. When he realized Willa had no desire to play an instrument or sing but loved music, he used their time together to play great music for her and to talk about the musicians and culture of Europe's great cities.

It was William Ducker, called Uncle Billy, who unlocked the treasury of Greek and Latin literature for Willa. An Englishman, he had at fifty come to Red Cloud with his family to open a store. He thought the local schools did not do enough for their pupils, and he gave his own children lessons in the classics. When he got to know Willa, he treated her as one of his own.

He thought she was a gifted girl, and he directed her reading so as to draw out the best in her. Even after she went off to the University of Nebraska, on her return home for vacations, she would go on reading poetry with Mr. Ducker. One day in the summer of 1893, she had just left his home when one of his children came running after her, crying out for help. She raced back to the house to find Mr. Ducker lying dead on the couch. Beside him was an open volume of the Greek classic, Homer's *Iliad*. Her grief at his passing was almost unbearable.

One of the state's most famous pioneers lived on the edge of Red Cloud, in its only elegant mansion. Silas Garber had risen from living in a sod hut as a child to becoming governor of Nebraska. He and his wife welcomed Willa into their home, where she met visiting notables who gave her a taste of the wider world beyond the prairie.

Silas Garber (left) and his wife, Lyra C. Wheeler Garber (right), pictured here in the early 1880s, lived in Red Cloud. During her high school years, Willa would visit them at their home and meet the interesting people who came to call.

Around their home was a cottonwood grove, where Willa often went to enjoy their picnics. The beautiful Lyra Garber was the belle of Red Cloud. She would figure in the Cather novel called *A Lost Lady*.

Music would always be central to Willa's life and work. Her natural feeling for it was encouraged by a neighbor, Mrs. Julia Miner. Born in Norway, the daughter of a professional musician, she was the wife of a Red Cloud merchant. In their parlor, she often played classical music for her three daughters and their close friend Willa Cather. In Cather's novel, *My Ántonia*, she describes a character patterned on Mrs. Miner as "short and square and sturdy looking. . . . Her face was rosy and solid, with bright twinkling eyes and a stubborn little chin. She was quick to anger, quick to laughter, and jolly from the depths of her soul." Cather once said she couldn't resist putting a little of Mrs. Miner in many of the mothers she portrayed.

Like small towns everywhere at that time, Red Cloud had what they called the Opera House, a room above a store. Every winter for a season of about six weeks, traveling companies would come to present plays, such as *The Count of Monte Cristo*, and operettas, such as *The Mikado*. Long after, Willa Cather wrote of these performances as one of the magical thrills of her youth. No movie, she said, could do for young people what those live performances of comedies and tragedies had done for her generation.

For one thing, it made Willa want to play roles herself. What was it like to be another person—male, female, young, old, nasty, lovable, ugly, or beautiful? When Willa was eleven, the Red Cloud paper noted that the recitation (in church) by Miss Willa Cather of Longfellow's poem *The Song of Hiawatha* "was particularly noticeable on account of its delivery which showed the little miss to be the possessor of extraordinary self-control and talent."

Willa was interested in acting at a young age. Here she is shown in her Hiawatha *recitation costume in the early 1880s.*

Willa wrote this poem on the cover of a scrapbook she made as a child. It is titled "Jack Jack." The first part reads: "This book was made by little Willie; When he was rather young and silly; He was of an artistic mind; And all his friends inside you'll find; This book made when he was a kid; Is the best thing he ever did."

Willa (back center, in top hat) *was part of the cast of* Beauty and the Beast *in Red Cloud in 1888. She played the father.*

In 1888 when a blizzard devastated Red Cloud, the children staged *Beauty and the Beast* at the Opera House to raise money for the needy. Willa played a merchant father so effectively that people were astonished to find it wasn't a boy in the role.

Books mattered too, of course. She read widely about the history of the trailbreakers who opened up the West, and she sampled stories that gave her fresh insights into what fiction could achieve. She pored over the novels appearing first in her own time—by George Eliot (the Englishwoman who used a man's name), Thomas Hardy, Rudyard Kipling, Robert Louis Stevenson and, of course, the Americans Nathaniel Hawthorne, Herman Melville, and Mark Twain.

But it was the life sciences at this time that fascinated her. When the family was still living in Virginia, a great-grandmother had insisted that Willa be bled once a month. Bloodletting, widely practiced at the time, was an old tradition that involved with-drawing blood from a patient in the misguided hope of purifying the blood in order to prevent or cure diseases. In school at Red Cloud, Willa studied biology and seemed to have inherited the old woman's set of bloodletting instruments. She used them to perform experi-mental vivisections, operating on animals such as toads and frogs.

Her interest in science and medicine was spurred by her close ties to Dr. G. E. McKeeby, the physician who took care of her fam-ily. His own daughter had died early, and Willa took her place in his affection. The experiments she carried out shocked the town, but that did not stop her. At her high school commencement in 1890, Willa—who was sixteen—gave an oration on the theme of "Superstition versus Investigation." In it she said:

> It is the most sacred right of man to investigate; we paid dearly for it in Eden; we have been shedding our heart's blood for it ever since. It is ours; we have bought it with a price.
>
> Scientific investigation is the hope of our age, as it must pre-cede all progress; and yet upon every hand we hear the objections to its pursuit. The boy who spends his time among the stones and flowers is a trifler, and if he tries with bungling attempt to pierce the mystery of animal life he is cruel. Of course if he becomes a great anatomist or a brilliant naturalist, his cruelties are forgotten or forgiven him; the world is very cautious, but it is generally safe to admire a man who has succeeded. We do not withhold from a few great scientists the right of the hospital, the post mortem or experimenting with animal life, but we are prone to think the right of experimenting with life too sacred a thing to be placed in the hands of inexperienced persons. Nevertheless, if we bar our novices from advancement, whence shall come our experts?

She challenged custom in still other ways. To the common concern voiced by the words "But what will the neighbors think?"

When she was in high school and into her second year of college,
Willa kept her hair short and often wore neckties and caps.

her answer was "I don't care." During her high school years, she cut her hair even shorter than most boys. She wore a starched white shirt, a necktie, and a derby hat or cap much like a boy's. (She would maintain this mode of dress until her second year in college.) Friends called her Willa or Willie, even though she'd ask them to call her Will. And in a friend's album, she identified herself as "Wm Cather MD."

Willa's behavior can be seen in part as an expression of the changing role of women at that time. The national magazines her family subscribed to carried accounts of the "New Woman" reaching for greater freedom and independence and for the chance to go beyond the ancient limits of motherhood and housekeeping. Get out in the world, go to the university, prepare for new kinds of work and responsibilities, campaign for women's right to vote, and hold even the highest offices.

CHAPTER THREE
Seeing Your Name in Print!

WILLA CATHER GRADUATED from Red Cloud High School in 1890, but could she go on to college? The expense was a problem for her father. Charles Cather had six children at this time, and he was hard pressed to make ends meet. But when he saw how eager Willa was to continue her studies, he borrowed the money to pay for her tuition, room and board, and books.

There was never any question that she would attend anyplace other than the University of Nebraska in Lincoln, the state capital. The city itself had only thirty thousand people. At this time, there were just four buildings in the university and about four hundred students. There were no dormitories as yet, so the students lived in boardinghouses. The faculty included several professors who would achieve great distinction in the years ahead.

Although the university was young and small, Cather soon found it offered courses by a number of very bright, promising instructors. Dorothy Canfield, for instance, later won a Pulitzer Prize for her novels. Alvin Johnson was later head of the New

Cather attended the University of Nebraska in Lincoln, shown here in 1892. While attending the university, she was a drama critic for the Nebraska State Journal.

School for Social Research in New York. Roscoe Pound was later dean of Harvard Law School in Cambridge, Massachusetts. Lieutenant John J. Pershing, a math and military science instructor, who would later be the general in command of U.S. forces in World War I (1914–1918).

When Cather applied, she was told she needed another year of schooling in certain subjects to meet the university requirements. So she tackled those subjects in the university's prep school with her usual energy. Very quickly, her teachers saw that she had a powerful will to succeed. Her aim was to concentrate on science courses—perhaps to become a doctor.

In the spring of 1891, one of those unexpected events occurred, the kind that can change the direction of someone's

Cather as a freshman at the University of Nebraska in Lincoln.

life. In her English course, the teacher asked the students to write a paper on Thomas Carlyle, a Scottish author who had died ten years earlier. Cather was already familiar with his writings on philosophy and history. She produced so special a work that, without telling her, the teacher submitted it to the *Nebraska State Journal.* Somehow it also got into the college literary magazine. Both printed her piece on the same day.

When Cather saw her writing and her name in print, she was stunned. Many years later, she recalled, "Up to that time I had planned to specialize in science. . . . I thought I would like to study medicine. But what youthful vanity can be unaffected by the sight of itself in print! It has a kind of hypnotic effect." She never forgot that essay. But she remembered it as the kind of flowery writing she detested, full of fancy figures of speech.

It didn't really discuss Carlyle himself, but rather the excitement and resentment against injustice that she felt on reading his book *The French Revolution: A History*. It had made her feel "so grown up to be bitter."

Several months later, the *Journal* printed another of her essays, this time on "Shakespeare and Hamlet." It probed the great friendship between Hamlet and Horatio. Deep friendship between individuals of the same sex was to become a theme in her *Death Comes for the Archbishop*—as well as a strong factor in her own life. The essay also examined the nature of art and what it takes to be an artist. Here the reader sees early signs of Cather's growing conviction that to be an artist was like committing yourself to a religion. You must follow wherever your art takes you, ready to sacrifice whatever in your personal life may stand in the way of creation. For a year, she was coeditor of a new literary magazine, the *Lasso*. When it folded, she joined the staff of another student magazine, the *Hesperian*, rising to managing editor in her junior year. And finally, as a senior, she edited her class yearbook, *Sombrero*.

By then Cather was busy writing short stories. The first of these, another English teacher liked so much that he sent it off to a Boston magazine, which printed it. She couldn't stop reworking this tale, called "Peter," and eight years later had it published again. It's the story of an old Bohemian violinist living with his family on the Nebraska prairie. Defeated by an unfulfilled musical life and in conflict with his practical farmer son, he commits suicide. It is a theme she would build on more than once.

Cather's stories, written when she was still so young, are grim portraits of life on the great prairie. Yet there was much she liked about those early years. It would be a long time before more mellow memories came to the surface.

In college years, students often make long-lasting friendships. But Cather's was not an outgoing personality, ready to embrace

In her later years at the University of Nebraska, Cather dressed more like the other women on campus and grew out her hair.

any and all. She did mix with students by joining dramatic, literary, and debating clubs. Yet at times, she felt lonely. In her second year, she stopped dressing like a man, let her hair grow, and began to look like the other campus women.

As she had done in Red Cloud, Cather made friends with several families in Lincoln. One was headed by Charles Gere, who was editor-publisher of the *Nebraska State Journal*. In 1893, early in her second year at the university, he asked her to write for his paper. She received one dollar for each column, and in the next three years, she produced more than three hundred pieces, many of them drama reviews.

This unexpected source of income came at a great time of need. Her father's real estate and loan business was in deep trouble. Luckily, her earnings managed to sustain her during the prolonged bad time.

Work as the *Journal's* drama critic won Cather broad fame. Theater companies with stars in the lead roles came into Lincoln frequently. Soon all became aware of this young critic sitting down front with a notepad in her lap. And when the review appeared the next day, it could be brilliant and witty, with clever praise for good work or biting sarcasm for bad.

Actors, singers, and writers of the highest standing would shiver in fearful anticipation of what this college kid would say about them in the paper. Cather expected all to give their best and had no tolerance if they failed. When some complained that

Cather works on an article at the Nebraska State Journal *in Lincoln in the mid-1890s. The photo was taken by Cather's friend Mariel Gere, daughter of Charles Gere, the editor-publisher of the newspaper.*

this fledgling never liked anything, she replied with a statistic: this season she had liked fourteen companies and damned only fifteen. So there!

By her last year at the university, Cather was getting tired. During the day, she attended a full round of academic courses. In the evening, she went to the theater and then hurried to the *Journal* office to write her review. Often she didn't get to bed till two o'clock in the morning.

Many years later, thinking back on her writing for the *Journal*, Cather said, "I was very fortunate in my first editor [Charles Gere]. He let me alone, knowing that I must work out my own

Cather worked for Charles Gere (left, in the late 1890s) *at the* Nebraska State Journal *while she was in college.*

salvation; and he was himself all that I was not and that I most admired. Isn't it too bad that after we are much older, and a little wiser, we cannot go back to those few vivid persons of our early youth and tell them how they have always remained with us, how much pleasure their fine personalities gave us, and give us to this very day."

Was Cather interested in politics—on campus or in the greater world? There's not much evidence of it, even though it was all around her. During her college years, the country began experiencing the worst economic crisis yet in its history. It started in 1893 and would last for five long years. It was a bitter disaster for workers, farmers, and the middle class. Rural and urban communities were devastated. When it struck, there were about 13 million families in the United States. Of these, 11 million had an average income of $380 a year. The richest 1 percent enjoyed wealth greater than the total remaining 99 percent. More than six hundred banks failed, and sixteen thousand businesses closed down.

Just before the economic collapse, a new People's Party (or Populist Party, as it was widely known) was launched at a convention in Omaha, Nebraska. Its platform was designed to appeal to workers and farmers alike. The preamble to the platform read:

> We meet in the midst of a nation brought to the verge of moral, political, and material ruin. . . . The fruits of the toil of millions are boldly stolen to build up colossal fortunes for a few, unprecedented in the history of mankind; and the possessors of these, in turn, despise the Republic and endanger liberty. From the same prolific womb of governmental injustice we breed the two great classes—paupers and millionaires.

Certainly Cather must have been aware of political issues because, while a student, she was welcomed many times into the

William Jennings Bryan (left) *and his wife, Mary Baird Bryan*
(right), *invited Cather to their Lincoln home when she was in college.*

home of William Jennings Bryan and his wife. In his early thir-
ties, Bryan had recently settled in Lincoln and won a seat in
Congress. Known ever after as a Nebraskan, he would campaign
for the presidency several times, advocating such issues as an
income tax and women's right to vote. There are echoes of him in
Cather's later fiction. In one of these stories, there is a child
named Bryan, after his father's hero. The boy learns that with that
name, he must grow up brave and unafraid of the dark.

Cather's record as a student was spotty. She was at her best in
English and the languages but spent only enough time in other
fields to get by. In her senior year, she did some practice teaching
as an aide to a professor who admired her writing.

That year she met Stephen Crane, only twenty-one at the time
but who had published in 1893 his first novel, *Maggie: A Girl of*

the *Streets*. Two years later, his next work, *The Red Badge of Courage*, appeared. That Civil War story had been run as a serial in the *Journal*.

Crane was the first recognized author Cather had met in person. It happened when he dropped into the *Journal* office around midnight. There, to his amazement, he saw a young woman—Willa Cather—standing but fast asleep! He nudged her awake, and they began talking. He was in Nebraska to report on the terrible drought devastating the farms in the West. In an article she wrote under another name years later, Cather recalled that Crane felt terribly frustrated about his work as a writer. It took so

Cather met author Stephen Crane (right) *in Lincoln in the mid-1890s. They remained friends until he died of tuberculosis in 1900 at the age of twenty-nine.*

awfully long to bring an idea for a story to the point of writing it. He said the detail of a thing had to filter through his blood, and then it came out like a native product, but it took forever. That meant there was little money in creating fiction. As for journalism, it's all hurry up and get it done, which he hated, but how else could a writer earn a living?

Soon after meeting Crane, an event even more important occurred. The Metropolitan Opera was performing in Chicago, Illinois, for a week. Together with the university librarian, Cather made the trip to savor her first taste of grand opera—and to see

Cather dressed in her wool coat and fancy hat while on a trip to Chicago to see the Metropolitan Opera in March 1895. The trip sparked a passion for opera and its divas that would continue throughout her life.

Cather graduated from the University of Nebraska in Lincoln in 1895, an unusual accomplishment for a woman in the late nine-teenth century. Here she poses in her graduation robe (left) *and in a fashionable gown* (right).

one of the United States' great cities for the first time. She would later use her impressions of that week in several of her novels.

At twenty-one, Cather's schooling was over. She would return to Red Cloud to try to earn a living as a journalist and to hole up nights in her room learning to write better.

CHAPTER FOUR
Married Nightingales Seldom Sing

WILLA CATHER FOUND THE RED CLOUD OF 1895 struggling to survive the economic depression. Her family was hit hard. Her father was now handling land titles and mortgages in Lincoln too, and banks he dealt with were in deep trouble. He tried desperately to hang on to the large tracts of heavily mortgaged land he'd acquired. Willa helped out in his home office, and her brothers Roscoe and Douglass, who taught school, helped as best they could.

She tried to reconnect with her old friends but found some had died and some had moved away. With people her own age, she felt uncomfortable. She wasn't quite the Willa who had gone off to university years ago. And hadn't those friends who stayed at home changed too?

The small success she'd earned by the publication of her writing made some people expect too much of her. Though she continued to write stories, she felt they were kid stuff, not the high quality she aimed for. How could they be better

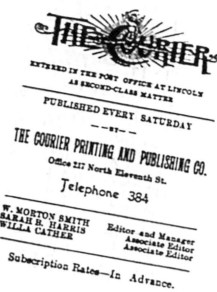

THE COURIER

ENTERED IN THE POST OFFICE AT LINCOLN
AS SECOND-CLASS MATTER

PUBLISHED EVERY SATURDAY
— —BY— —

THE COURIER PRINTING AND PUBLISHING CO.
Office 217 North Eleventh St.

Telephone 384

W. MORTON SMITH   Editor and Manager
SARAH B. HARRIS   Associate Editor
WILLA CATHER   Associate Editor

Subscription Rates—In Advance.

After college, Cather got a job working for Sarah Harris (left) *at the* Lincoln Courier (cover from September 7, 1895, pictured above).

when she knew so little of the world? She thought of Stephen Crane and the much richer experience that lay behind his achievements.

Prospects improved when Sarah Harris, an older friend she'd made while at the university, offered her work on the *Lincoln Courier*. Harris was editor and part-owner of the paper. Cather moved back to Lincoln to write a column and drama reviews.

Mrs. Harris was a freethinker, one who formed her opinions from reason rather than by authority or convention. Through her paper, she carried on fierce political campaigns. As a drama critic, Cather wrote not only reviews but articles on acting and playwriting. Her work was considered original and challenging. But for unknown reasons, within a few months, things went wrong, and by the winter, Cather was back in Red Cloud.

Another chance to escape Red Cloud came when an English professor abruptly resigned from the University of Nebraska. Cather wanted desperately to replace him. But the English department head, whose views she had openly opposed while a student, said absolutely not. Biographers of Cather believe she was fortunate to be turned down. Had she been given the job, she probably would have stayed on permanently. And leading a life as an academic would have so narrowly limited her experience that it would have made for a different novelist—and a much lesser one.

Still, Cather managed to visit Lincoln now and then, happy to see old friends. One lucky evening, she was dining with the Geres where she met Charles Axtell, a Pittsburgh publisher of farm journals. When the conversation turned to journalism, Axtell was impressed by Cather's grasp of the field—and, of course, by Gere's praise of her work for the *Journal*. In the spring of 1896, Axtell offered her a job. He had taken over a family magazine and renamed it the *Home Monthly*. Would she become the editor?

To be an editor! And in a big city! It promised economic security, enjoyment of the arts, and connection to all sorts of interesting people. She couldn't say yes quickly enough.

In June 1896, Cather moved to Pittsburgh, in western Pennsylvania. She would never again live in Nebraska, although she would continue to visit her family there. Pittsburgh, with about three hundred thousand people, was built where the Allegheny and Monongahela rivers join to form the Ohio River. Giant steel mills belched fire and smoke into the skies day and night. Coming from the flat, dry plains, Cather found the broad rivers and green hills helped her overlook the industrial monstrosities. The enterprise and labor of untold thousands of underpaid workers had created great fortunes for the city's elite—Andrew Carnegie, Henry

A view of Union Station (center) *in Pittsburgh, Pennsylvania, in the early 1900s. Cather moved to Pittsburgh in 1896 and would later teach at Central High School, the building in the distance behind the smokestack at right.*

Clay Frick, Henry J. Heinz, Andrew W. Mellon, and the Schenleys. Monuments, parks, museums, libraries, theaters, and concert halls bore the names of the wealthy and would provide pleasures of which Cather would take full advantage.

But Pittsburgh was more than the home of the rich and respectable. Immigrant working-class neighborhoods were criss-crossed with groceries, tobacco shops, saloons, gambling dens, pool halls, and ballparks. Theater productions featured working-class values and were spiced by references to local celebrities and events.

Music was the art Cather loved most. She would bring home one of Pittsburgh composer Ethelbert Nevin's new pieces to have a friend play it for her on the piano. Richard Wagner was one of her favorite composers, though she joked that the power of his sound was not so effective in Pittsburgh, where everyone was used to the noise of the iron mills.

When she first heard Antonin Dvorak's *New World* Symphony (Symphony #9), she wrote that the largo (slow tempo) movement made her see "the limitless prairies, full of the peasantry of all nations of Europe . . . and it seems as though from each of those far scattered lights that at night mark the dwellings of these people of the plains, there comes the song of a homesick heart."

In the opinion of Edith Lewis, soon to become Cather's long-time companion, music was "an emotional experience that had a potent influence on her own imaginative processes—quickening the flow of her ideas, suggesting new forms and associations, translating itself into parallel movements of thought and feeling. . . . Her style, her beauty of cadence and rhythm were the result of a transposed musical feeling, and were arrived at almost unconsciously, instead of being a conscious effort to produce definite effects with words." You can see in several of her novels the often major role music and musicians play.

The Axtells invited Cather to stay with them until she could find a place of her own. They were a kindly and conservative family devoted to church work. For diversion, she looked to George Gerwig's family. He had been a drama critic in Lincoln when they first met, and he was head of Pittsburgh's board of education. Mrs. Gerwig introduced Cather to her elite women's club. When Cather was invited to give an impromptu talk, her essay on Thomas Carlyle flashed into her mind. She remembered it almost word for word, and she astonished her audience with an impassioned delivery. They thought that she had made it all up as she went along. The event made her a celebrity in Pittsburgh. Everyone, it seemed, was eager to invite her to their homes.

Several weeks later, Cather left the Axtells for a room she found in a boardinghouse in a decent neighborhood. It was not too far from the magazine's office, and she went to and from work on a

In late 1896, Cather moved into a boardinghouse in Pittsburgh that was near the newly opened Carnegie Library (above). *The library was part of the Carnegie Institute, which eventually would include an art gallery, natural history museum, and concert hall.*

bicycle, racing the electric streetcar all the way. Confident they could rely on their young editor, the Axtells left for a long vacation.

Cather found that editing a family magazine wasn't all that exciting. Find material about running a neat home, cooking, gardening, sewing, and raising babies? What fun was that? And she had to do it almost all by herself.

But she made the best of it. Some of the pieces in her first issue she wrote herself, signing a made-up woman's name to one or a man's to another. She fretted over writing so much of the magazine herself, for it denied other professional authors that income. Yet she couldn't resist seeing her own work in print, even without her name on it.

For her second issue, she featured an article on the wives of the two leading presidential candidates, Mrs. William McKinley and

Mrs. William Jennings Bryan. She did extensive research, secured the photos, and wrote the piece herself, using a pen name. Never a political activist, Cather did not advocate for either candidate. In the end, the Republican McKinley defeated the Democrat Bryan.

Her new friends took Cather on picnics, boat rides, and excursions, including a visit to nearby Homestead. Only a few years before, Henry Clay Frick and Andrew Carnegie, who owned the huge steel mills there, had smashed the labor union in a long bloody struggle. Thousands of workers were now putting in seven-day weeks of twelve-hour shifts at reduced wages, with only two days a year off—Christmas and the Fourth of July. What Cather thought of it, we don't know.

Not long after taking on the new job, Cather accepted part-time work as drama critic of the *Pittsburgh Daily Leader*. She could reenter the theatrical world she had enjoyed so much in Lincoln.

One wonders how she managed to keep writing fiction all this time. Yet in the year she edited the *Home Monthly*, seven of her stories appeared in the magazine. Most were just fillers. But at least two were of such quality they raised the interest of New York editors. One offered her one hundred dollars for a story, but she turned him down because she needed it for her own magazine. But it caused her to think that perhaps she could make it in the grand world of New York publishing.

By early 1897, Cather had made such a strong impression on the town that the *Pittsburgh Press* sent a reporter to interview her. She gave that reporter more than the plain facts. Sometimes she embroidered them. Readers were told that Miss Willa Cather

is such a thoroughly up-to-date woman she certainly should be mentioned among the pioneers in woman's advancement. . . . Miss Cather is just beginning her career, but she is doing it with the true progressive, western spirit, that fears neither responsibility nor work, and it will be a career worth watching. To go off, when one is but twenty-one [not her true age] into an entirely new part of the country and undertake to establish and edit a new magazine requires plenty of 'grit'—a quality as valuable in a business woman as in a business man.

Cather clipped the article and mailed it to her parents.

With the end of her first year on the *Home Monthly*, Cather took off for a vacation in Red Cloud. While she was away, the magazine was sold to another publishing house. And she was out of a job. Then came a message from the *Pittsburgh Leader*. It wanted her to come on staff as assistant wire service editor, at seventy-five dollars a month, plus extra money for writing reviews and articles. It was a great break—an even better job. In September 1897, she reported for work at the newspaper.

Cather was nearly twenty-four. Many young women of that age were married. Cather dated often in Pittsburgh, and one young doctor had proposed to her. She liked him but marriage? No. Then another possibility came along—an English teacher at nearby Allegheny High School. Theirs was a warm friendship, but she didn't want to transform it into marriage. She told a friend she liked her freedom and her independence too much to be tied down. And it is likely that though she had male friends throughout her life, she did not find men sexually attractive. It seems the males she loved most dearly were her father and her older brothers Douglass and Roscoe. She loved her younger brothers too, but she was more like an aunt to them than a sister. However, there were many women in her life with whom she would form intense attachments.

In more than one work, Cather wrote that in her view art and marriage were not a good match. The writer, the painter, and the composer—they needed solitude and the freedom to do, go, or create when they pleased. Writing once of an opera singer who quit the stage to marry, Cather said the artist must love his art above all things. And added, "Married nightingales seldom sing." She expressed that conviction in her fiction, where happily married artists never appear. She instructed her characters to avoid marriage or if you make the mistake, then expect to suffer for it. She went out of her way once to distort the marriage of a close friend in one of her writings. He was Ethelbert Nevin, a composer she had met in Pittsburgh. Although Nevin was happy in his real marriage, her fictional composer's marriage ends in disaster.

George Seibel, a young freelance journalist, and his wife soon became Cather's close friends. They would meet in the Seibel home for weekly readings of modern and classical French authors, finishing the talk with supper. Cather spent every Christmas with them and remained close even after moving away.

Pittsburgh was big enough and certainly rich enough to support its own theater, the Pittsburgh Stock Company. The star actress was Mrs. Lizzie Collier, a charming woman Cather had met in the course of her theater reviewing. One evening, the actress introduced Cather to a friend, Isabelle McClung. Described as tall and handsome, McClung was the daughter of one of the city's leading families. Her father, conservative judge Samuel A. McClung, had recently presided over the trial of Alexander Berkman, an anarchist who had tried to kill Henry Clay Frick, head of the Carnegie steelworks in nearby Homestead. Upon the jury's verdict of guilty, Judge McClung had sentenced Berkman to the maximum term of twenty-two years in prison.

The two young women felt an immediate bond. Isabelle McClung thought Pittsburgh was a dull, stuffy town. She needed diversion and found it in pursuing the arts. She made friends with performers in music and theater and, when Cather came into the picture, instantly took to her as an extraordinary woman of her own age who could transform everyday life. So began an intimate friendship "that grew into a great love that lasted a lifetime,"

In 1897 Cather met Isabelle McClung, daughter of a wealthy, conservative judge in Pittsburgh and member of the city's social elite.

according to Cather biographer James Woodress. Two years later, McClung would invite Cather to come live in her home. It was a spacious mansion, a far cry from Cather's boardinghouse, and in the elegant part of town. When McClung told her family what she wished to do, they were appalled. Who was this Cather woman? Why would their properly brought up daughter want to live with her? They said she couldn't do this. McClung's reply was that either Miss Cather would live there or she would leave home.

Her parents gave in—but on the condition that the living arrangement be temporary. It wasn't. Cather stayed for the next five years. Her new home was staffed by servants. Elaborate dinners

Cather lived at the McClung house in Pittsburgh with Isabelle McClung for many years.

were served, often with distinguished guests at the table. Elizabeth Moorhead, a friend of both, wrote that after dinner the two young women "would go upstairs to the bedroom they shared to read together in quiet. . . . Here the friends spent many happy and fruitful hours." To provide Cather with privacy for her writing, McClung fixed up a former sewing room in the attic. There her friend could write undisturbed.

Was Cather's relationship with McClung sexual? If it was, it's understandable that they would have tried to conceal it because of the stigma attached to lesbianism at that time. But as Janis P. Stout puts it in her biography of Cather, "In a way, though, it does not matter whether the relationship of Cather and McClung was physically lesbian, since it is absolutely clear that it was emotionally so. They were devoted to each other."

CHAPTER FIVE
Teacher and Traveler

WHILE CATHER'S LIFE OUTSIDE OF WORK was going very well, her professional life became increasingly rigorous during her years in Pittsburgh. Her job at the *Leader* expanded mightily when, in February 1898, the U.S. battleship the *Maine* exploded in the Havana, Cuba, harbor. The U.S. Congress blamed Spain, which ruled Cuba, and thus declared war on Spain. Dispatches poured in to Cather's telegraph desk at the newspaper. The "splendid little war," as a secretary of state, John Milton Hay, would later call it, was swiftly over.

Spain gave up Cuba, and the United States occupied the island. The United States also won from Spain the Caribbean island of Puerto Rico and in the Pacific the island of Guam and all the Philippines. The victory of Admiral George Dewey over Spain brought the annexation of Hawaii.

That was a lot of news to cover. And it evoked intense public debate over its significance for the United States. Many Americans thought of their country as a righteous nation always on the side

Cather (center) *reads to her brother Jack* (left) *and sister Elsie* (right) *during a trip to Red Cloud in 1900. Cather often visited her family, even after moving away from Nebraska.*

of the angels. But was it now traveling the same path to empire as the much older nations of Europe? What Cather's answer might have been is not known. She left no record. Other writers—Mark Twain, for instance—made their views clear. In a national magazine, the author of *Huckleberry Finn* published a savage condemnation of the United States' pirate raid of the Philippines.

Even with this added burden, Cather continued to write stories and to take on freelance assignments for newspapers and magazines. She would use her own name, a pseudonym, or no byline. She also traveled—home to Nebraska and on vacations to New York or Washington, D.C.

In the spring of 1900, Cather felt she'd had more than enough of the world of journalism. That job would get her nowhere as a real writer. Yet there's no doubt that journalism was the trade in which she learned to master her skills. One can recognize her distinctive voice in the huge pile of nonfiction writing done for newspapers and magazines. And that was not all. In the period between 1892 and 1902, twenty-seven of her short stories were published.

She knew she had a gift and that it needed time and attention. Teaching would at least provide three months of freedom every summer, and she believed she'd like it. From very early on, she'd had warm relationships with children, beginning with the six Cather siblings who came after her. That connection with children would continue all her life.

Through her friendship with George Gerwig, Cather secured a job teaching Latin at Central High School. She was now twenty-seven years old. Her pay would be less, only $650 a year, but with free lodging at the McClungs, she needed less. Her Latin was so rusty that she gladly switched to teaching English after the first semester. After two years at Central, she transferred to Allegheny High School and remained there for the next three years. By the time she left in 1906, her salary had advanced to $1,300 a year.

Cather's classroom attire consisted mainly of shirtwaists with collar and cuffs. Men's ties, too, were a continuing habit. Students

Students recalled Cather as a stimulating teacher, always interested in what they were doing and thinking.

remembered her as a good-looking woman, a bit plump, who wore her hair parted in the middle and held in a bun at the back. She often invited students to come for tea with her at the McClung home.

Her students recalled that she insisted the only way to learn to write was to write, not just talk about it. She had them write a short piece for about ten or fifteen minutes each day, when the English class began. Her standard for achievement was high. Only a few got a grade of 85 percent. Most got 70s. But every paper was carefully corrected and returned. If a student over-reached in a studied attempt to produce elegant prose, her negative response was quick and firm. The result? Those who did well thought Miss Cather was great. The others detested her.

In the summer of 1902, Willa Cather and Isabelle McClung went to Europe together for the first time. They spent five weeks in London, England, and five more in Paris, France, with side

Cather sits aboard the SS Nordland *with a young girl as the ship set sail for Great Britain in June 1902. Cather would use the trip to visit the birthplaces and graves of artists whom she admired.*

This photo of Cather in Europe is from her scrapbook of her first trip overseas in 1902.

trips to other regions of each country. Cather's impressions of her sightseeing were voiced in a series of columns she sent to the *Lincoln State Journal*.

A highlight of sightseeing in Great Britain was a visit to A. E. Housman, the British scholar and poet. Learning that he lived in a suburb north of London, the two women, joined by their friend Dorothy Canfield, took a bus out to Highgate. They were astonished to find Housman, a bachelor, living in a ramshackle boardinghouse in a dreary area. Cather had read Housman's *A Shropshire Lad*, his first volume of poetry, when it appeared, and loved his magical lyrics. When she tried to tell him what poems such as "When I Was Young and Twenty" meant to her, he was flustered, not knowing what to say. In Britain, it seemed, one didn't just knock unannounced at a stranger's door and expect to be welcomed warmly.

But their embarrassment faded when Canfield told Housman she was working on a doctoral dissertation on how the French dramatists Pierre Corneille and Jean Racine were viewed in Great Britain. Anything scholarly interested Housman, and he and Canfield carried on while "Willa sat on his couch with broken springs, brooding about Housman's shoes and cuffs and shabby carpet and wondering how the gaunt and gray and embittered figure before her could have written the magical lyrics that had moved her so deeply."

Cather's own collection of verse, *April Twilights*, was published in 1903. Readers thought few of the poems were worth remembering. They were mostly imitative, fumbling for an original, true voice. The better poems she wrote were added in later editions (1923 and 1933) of *April Twilights*. She once said, "I do not take myself seriously as a poet."

A month after the poetry volume appeared, S. S. McClure, the publisher of *McClure's Magazine*, asked Cather to meet him in New York. He'd heard about this talented young woman through one of her old friends in Nebraska. When he asked his staff about her, he learned they had turned down several of her stories, but a few were still in the office. He read them himself, liked them, and wired her to come in.

Cather met with McClure at his office on West Twenty-third Street in Manhattan in May 1903. She found him to be a restless little man, blue-eyed and bursting with energy. His impression of her was of a stocky young woman fresh from country living. He fired questions at her in order to learn all he could about her personal history. She opened up to this stranger as though he were an old friend. And after two hours, he said he'd print her stories in his magazine and then publish them in a book.

It was a magical meeting. She came out of it feeling like a woman reborn. She could do anything—for him as well as herself! She believed if S. S. McClure were a preacher, he'd have the congregation ready to die for him.

There were more talks with McClure and then a visit to his home, where she met his wife. Cather went back to Pittsburgh convinced that her literary career was at last launched. Over the next two years, his magazine published some of her stories.

That summer of 1903, Cather returned to Nebraska on vacation. There she met a Lincoln woman, Edith Lewis, a recent graduate of Smith, an elite Massachusetts all-women's college.

She described seeing Cather as "a rather slim figure, in a grey and white striped cotton dress, sitting very upright in a straight-backed chair. She had curling chestnut-brown hair,

Cather met Edith Lewis (right, in the mid-1920s) *on a trip to Nebraska in 1903. Lewis, also from Nebraska, would become Cather's lifelong friend and companion. Employed in publishing, Lewis would also become the copy editor, proofreader, and editor of Cather's works.*

done high on her head, a fair skin; but the feature one noticed particularly was her eyes. They were dark blue eyes, with dark lashes; and I know no way of describing them except to say that they were the eyes of genius."

Lewis knew of Cather's success in the literary world and was in awe of her. Lewis was about to start work with the Century Company, a publishing firm in New York. Over the next two years, when Cather came to New York, Lewis would put her up in her studio apartment.

In 1905 McClure's book publishing firm issued *The Troll Garden*, containing seven of her stories. Cather dedicated her book to Isabelle McClung. Several of the stories in *The Troll Garden* reflect life on the prairie. Some of the tales are amateurish. Others show a degree of progress in her writing. Several suggest the fallacy of the popular belief in rigid male and female roles. Characteristics believed true only of the male, she gives to the female and vice versa. A girl is shown heroically riding 25 miles (40 km) uphill on her bike to save a bank from financial ruin. (Women were not regarded as either athletic or heroic in the early 1900s.) And in another story, we see a man's hands as white as a girl's, while his sister comes off as the more masculine of the two. Cather most often portrayed a male as the chief character in her stories, an unusual choice for a female author.

O Pioneers! a novel that would appear eight years later, reveals her deep love for the Nebraska countryside. Yet in *The Troll Garden*, the reader feels how dismal and how deadening life on the prairie can be. Characters go mad when prolonged drought ruins their crops. Others commit suicide. Of course, these stories infuriated Nebraskans. And when readers recognized family members or neighbors in negatively portrayed characters, they sent her angry letters. Those characters portrayed as artists come off somewhat better, with some portrayed as insufferable egotists,

Writing and Rewriting

The story "A Death in the Desert" is a remarkable example of the intensive care Willa Cather gave to her fiction in her desire to do her best. First printed in *Scribner's Magazine*, it was to be reprinted in *The Troll Garden* collection. But Cather made 148 substantive changes to it, both large and small, slicing off about a thousand words. When she reprinted the story again in the volume *Youth and the Bright Medusa* (1920), she reworked it still another time. She made 184 significant changes and cut it by two-thirds of its original length. Still not satisfied, she refused to have it reprinted many years later in her collected works.

while others are seen as victims of society matrons who prey upon celebrities.

Cather was aware that her writing was far from the best. As she told a friend, what she had done up to then was "half real and half an imitation." The poor sales of *The Troll Garden* bitterly disappointed her. When interviewed by a Lincoln newspaper, she said local readers had wanted her to write propaganda to promote the town.

CHAPTER SIX
A Challenge in New York

SOON AFTER *THE TROLL GARDEN* appeared, Cather and McClung spent two months visiting in the West. They dropped in on Cather's brothers Douglass and Roscoe and stopped for a while with her parents in their new home in Red Cloud. Then it was back to Pittsburgh and teaching.

In the spring of 1906, McClure suddenly popped up in Pittsburgh to offer Cather an editing job on his *McClure's Magazine*. Considering how rare it was at that time—more than one hundred years ago—for a woman to hold a position as editor on such a prestigious magazine, why did McClure do this? In addition to recognizing her talent, perhaps it was because he thought that an unmarried woman, without a home and family to command all her attention, would be glad to devote herself completely to her work.

It was ten years now that Cather had lived in Pittsburgh. She had a secure job teaching and a home with the McClungs. But the personal magnetism of McClure, the experience she would gain

Cather and Isabelle McClung (pictured here with an unknown man) spent time in the western United States in 1905. They visited Cather's brothers Douglass and Roscoe and also stopped in Red Cloud to visit her parents.

on one of the country's leading magazines, and the allure of a great city—all must have led her to leave Pittsburgh for this challenging new job.

McClure had founded his magazine in 1890, and by now it was rated the most exciting of all general magazines. Its editorial approach was daring, the quality of its writing excellent, and its impact upon the times without parallel.

Behind it all was that erratic genius, S. S. McClure. A poor Irish immigrant, he had worked his way through college, married, launched a newspaper syndicate, and then created *McClure's Magazine.* A few years before now, he had moved the magazine into what President Theodore Roosevelt called

S. S. McClure (left) *offered Cather a job at his popular magazine,* McClure's, *in 1906. In addition to introducing the works of many unknown writers, his magazine also published articles by the muckrakers, a group who exposed social ills through journalism.*

muckraking. That is, he had commissioned talented writers to dig up dirt on graft, corruption, greed, and fakery in big business and in government. Writers were offered a high fee and asked to give all the time necessary to the most thorough research and then to write their findings in reports that ran as a serial in issue after issue. Ida Tarbell had provided sensational work on John D. Rockefeller's Standard Oil Company. Lincoln Steffens had exposed corruption in half a dozen cities and half a dozen states. Ray Stannard Baker had probed the criminality of the way railroads operated across the country.

But that was not the magazine's only distinction. *McClure's* printed the fiction of Thomas Hardy, Rudyard Kipling, Stephen

Crane, O. Henry, Jack London, Mark Twain, Arthur Conan Doyle, Robert Louis Stevenson, and Joseph Conrad—indicating it was not only great reporters but great storytellers that *McClure's* looked for and published.

Preparing to go to New York, Cather once more read the draft of a novel she'd finished. Then she tore the manuscript into pieces and tossed it into her wastebasket. "It wasn't good enough," she told an interviewer long after. That interviewer wondered, "But would any of the rest of us have had the faith in our own judgment to make that decision—and the ruthlessness to execute sentence on our own work!"

Arriving in New York, Cather moved into a studio apartment at 60 Washington Square South, which she shared with Edith Lewis, now working as a proofreader at *McClure's*. It was on the top floor of an old house, facing Washington Square, the center of Greenwich Village life. There were still horse-drawn stage-coaches as well as the new buses running on Fifth Avenue, which ended at the square.

Cather began as an associate editor. Her duties included reading the manuscripts that flooded in from hopeful writers. Most were impossible. Others dealt with issues the magazine wanted to pursue, but the writing needed thorough editing.

Cather would tell hopeful writers, "Unless you have something in you so fierce that it simply pours itself out in a torrent, heedless of rules or bounds—then do not bother to write anything at all. Why should you? The time for revision is after a thing is on paper—not before."

Her work at the office left her little time or energy for her own writing. She did manage to publish four short stories during her five years at the magazine. She never reprinted them. Only after her death did they appear in her *Collected Short Stories*.

About six months after she'd been on staff, McClure assigned her to a task that would send her to Boston for more than a year.

For Hopeful Writers

In a collection of her letters, notes, and essays on writing as an art, Willa Cather had much to say of great value to anyone who aspires to create fiction. Here are a few passages from that volume:

> Every great story must leave in the mind of the sensitive reader an intangible residuum of pleasure; a cadence, a quality of voice that is exclusively the writer's own, individual, unique. A quality that one can remember without the volume at hand, can experience over and over again in the mind but can never absolutely define, as one can experience in memory a melody, or the summer perfume of a garden. The magnitude of the subject-matter is not of primary importance. . . .

Throughout her life, Cather thought about the art and the craft of writing. Several decades of her observations would be later compiled in a book titled Willa Cather on Writing: Critical Studies on Writing as an Art, *published in 1949, two years after her death.*

* * *

If he [a writer] achieves anything noble, anything enduring, it must be by giving himself absolutely to his material. And this gift of sympathy is his great gift; it is the fine thing in him that alone can make his work fine. He fades away into the land and people of his heart, he dies of love only to be born again. The artist spends a lifetime in loving the things that haunt him, in having his mind "teased" by them, in trying to get these conceptions down on paper exactly as they are to him and not in conventional poses supposed to reveal their character.

* * *

To note an artist's limitations is but to define his genius. A reporter can write equally well about everything that is presented to his view, but a creative writer can do his best only with what lies within the range and character of his talent.

* * *

Art, it seems to me, should simplify. That, indeed, is very nearly the whole of the higher artistic process; finding what conventions of form and what detail one can do without and yet preserve the spirit of the whole—so that all that one has suppressed and cut away is there to the reader's consciousness as much as if it were in type on the page. Millet had done hundreds of sketches of peasants sowing grain, some of them very complicated and interesting, but when he came to paint the spirit of them all into one picture, "The Sower," the composition is so simple that it seems inevitable. All the discarded sketches that went before made the picture what it finally became, and the process was all the time one of simplifying many conceptions good in themselves for one that was better and more universal.

He had bought writer Georgine Milmine's manuscript *The Life of Mary Baker G. Eddy*, the woman who founded the Church of Christ, Scientist [Christian Science] twenty-five years earlier. But Milmine's narrative was so disorganized and her claims so unsubstantiated that the manuscript needed better writing and additional research.

Cather took on the task, meeting with Milmine, moving about New England to interview sources, and checking facts. Christian Science was a subject requiring the greatest care, as it was a relatively new but controversial denomination of Christianity, with many important followers.

She worked very hard. The assignment was even more demanding than expected. When completed, the series ran in fifteen installments, stretching well beyond a year. Although most of the writing was recognizably Cather's, the magazine kept Milmine's name as author. That was fortunate, for the series infuriated the Christian Science church, and Cather was spared their attacks.

While in Boston, Cather managed to meet new friends. One of them, a young Houghton Mifflin editor, described Cather as "a fresh-faced, broad-browed, plain-speaking young woman, standing her ground with a singular solidity."

And then there was Alice Brandeis, the wife of an eminent lawyer, Louis D. Brandeis, who later served on the U.S. Supreme Court. Mrs. Brandeis introduced Cather to Annie Fields, the nearly eighty-year-old widow of James T. Fields. His firm, Ticknor & Fields, had published the United States' and Great Britain's finest authors, many of whom had been guests in the Fields's Charles Street home. The living room held precious mementos of the authors who had been guests there. There was a lock of hair from British poet John Keats and the manuscripts of several writers Cather cherished.

On Cather's first visit to Mrs. Fields, she met an author twenty-five years her senior whom she had long admired—Sarah

Cather had admired author Sarah Orne Jewett (right) *long before they met. Jewett's books were all centered on the small town in Maine where she grew up.*

Orne Jewett. (Cather would be her last new friend, for Jewett would die only sixteen months after this meeting.) Each of the two writers had grown up in a small town at a time when their economies were breaking apart and old customs and beliefs fading. When young, both had cherished connections to older folk. And both had enjoyed the same poets and novelists. Each had started writing while still in school and published their first stories when still in their teens. Their meeting was one of those unpredictable, chance events in life that can mean so much.

Cather was made managing editor at McClure's in 1907. The necklace she is wearing in this photograph was a gift given to her by her friend Sarah Orne Jewett.

Jewett, a doctor's daughter, was a novelist and writer of regional short stories. Her first novel was published when she was thirty-five. Several collections of short stories followed, and then came the work she is best remembered for, *The Country of the Pointed Firs* (1896). She had stopped writing in 1902, after an incapacitating accident. For nearly thirty years, she and Annie Fields had been intimate friends, traveling together in Europe several times and spending summers and winters in each other's homes.

Jewett's narratives of life in New England and her contrast of the older generation with the new and the past with the present continued the earlier regional tradition of Harriet Beecher Stowe, whose portrayal of slavery in *Uncle Tom's Cabin* (1852) helped spark the U.S. Civil War. One of Jewett's major themes dealt with women's friendships—as schoolgirls, older women, and relatives. Her work was infused with kindness and humor. By the time she and Cather met, Jewett was esteemed as the foremost regional writer of the century just ended. In Cather's opinion, Jewett ranked with the great American writers Mark Twain and Henry James.

When Cather returned to the office in New York, she was given the title of managing editor. Actually, McClure himself made the major decisions. Still, she would learn a great deal from this far more experienced editor during the three years she held that title.

CHAPTER SEVEN
To Write about Life, You Must Live It

IN THE SPRING OF 1908, Cather and McClung sailed off to Europe again, this time to visit Italy. When they returned to New York, Cather went up to Maine to visit Annie Fields and Sarah Orne Jewett. It was on her return to New York that Cather, with Edith Lewis, rented an apartment at 82 Washington Place. They would continue to live together for the rest of Cather's life. One of their friends, Elizabeth Sergeant, said of their relationship, "A captain . . . must have a first officer, who does a lot the captain never knows about to steer the boat through the rocks and reefs."

A political liberal, Sergeant wrote articles about social issues, such as the need to provide low-cost housing for the poor. Cather bought them for *McClure's*. Though no activist herself, she formed a warm relationship with Sergeant.

Cather and Jewett corresponded often. When Jewett read Cather's stories as they appeared in the magazine, she would send her opinion of them, trying to be helpful to the younger writer. She noted in

one letter how Cather often told stories in the voice of a man. She
held it to be a mistake, a masquerade, for a woman to write in the
character of the male. Better to write *about* the male than to try to *be*
the male. But Cather couldn't accept that. She'd written from the
male point of view several times and would go on doing so. Yet most
critics believe the best characters she would create were female.

Jewett wrote Cather another letter late in 1908, in which she
warned that Cather's magazine editing work was hampering her
creative writing:

> I cannot help saying what I think about your writing and its
> being hindered by such incessant, important, responsible work
> as you have in your hands now. I do think that it is impossible
> for you to work so hard and yet have your gifts mature as they
> should—when one's first working power has spent itself, noth-
> ing ever brings it back just the same. . . . If you don't keep and
> guard and mature your force and, above all, have time and
> quiet to perfect your work, you will be writing things not much
> better than you did five years ago. . . . Your vivid, exciting com-
> panionship in the office must not be your audience, you must
> find your own quiet center of life and write from that to the
> world that holds offices, and all society . . . in short, you must
> write to the human heart, the great consciousness that all
> humanity goes to make up. Otherwise what might be strength
> in a writer is only crudeness, and what might be insight is only
> observation; sentiment falls to sentimentality—you can write
> about life, but never life itself. To work in silence and with all
> one's heart, that is the writer's lot; he is the only artist who must
> be solitary, and yet needs the widest outlook upon the world.

To write about life, you must live it. . . . That truth struck
home. Cather was not living even half a life as a writer. She was
devoting almost all her time and her energy to the day-to-day

work of putting out the magazine. What strength was left for her prime concern—to write fiction about life as she saw it and felt it? But how could she give up her job? What would she live on? She was doing her best to send money to her family and to save for the day when she could afford to leave *McClure's*.

She poured out her feelings in an eight-page letter to Jewett. Cather knew that her friend was right. Her literary career had been virtually stalled during these two and a half years on the magazine. Yet she couldn't slack off to squeeze out time for her own writing. While she stayed on the payroll, she had to give her best in shaping the kind of journalism *McClure's* prided itself on.

And, in fact, her boss valued her excellent editorial work and paid her generously for it.

When Jewett died unexpectedly in June 1909, Cather was devastated. Perhaps sensing her despair and as a big bonus, McClure sent her to Europe to scout for talented writers and stories. On her 1909 trip to London, she met luminaries such as Lady Augusta Gregory, who, with W. B. Yeats, founded

Cather poses in a formal gown when she worked for McClure's.

Ireland's Abbey Theater; and novelists H. G. Wells, John Galsworthy, and Thomas Hardy. She returned to the office with manuscripts aplenty.

By the end of the year, Cather was so tired—and missed her friend so deeply—that she spent the Christmas holiday season in bed. As 1910 arrived, McClure left for Europe, placing Cather in complete charge of the magazine. Its circulation under her guiding hand averaged 400,000 copies per month, and its income from advertising was greater than that of any other magazine.

Early in 1911, Cather fell sick with a sudden, frightening illness. It proved to be mastoiditis, a bacterial infection of the bone behind the ear. The pain was persistent and throbbing. Antibiotic treatment was unknown then, and Cather suffered in the hospital for several weeks.

As she regained her health, she was able to visit Boston on business and took time to see her friends again. During the summer months, she also came up with an idea for a novel. She hoped if it were good enough, *McClure's* would publish it as a serial. But before the year was out, a financial reorganization of the magazine took place, and McClure lost control. That crucial change triggered Cather's decision to quit editorial work but not to sever her connection to the magazine. That would continue until the middle of 1913.

She had given six years to a magazine whose power as a muckraker had made a significant difference in U.S. political and economic life. Cather herself was never a crusader for reform. Her values would be found in the stories she created and the characters she brought to life. And this is what she turned to now.

She needed time to clear her mind of the infinite number of decisions she had been obliged to make day after day at the magazine. Despite all that, somehow she managed to write the first installment of a novel, *Alexander's Bridge*, that *McClure's* began to publish serially. On the strength of that first installment, Houghton Mifflin agreed to publish the complete novel.

CHAPTER EIGHT
Cliff Dwellers— and Pioneers

HER FIRST NOVEL, CATHER SAID, was about a bridge builder with a double nature. She had recalled the news event of 1907 about a bridge under construction on the Canadian side of the Saint Lawrence River that had collapsed, killing about a hundred workers. The engineer who designed the bridge was blamed for neglect. It was said he had given in to pressure to go ahead, when he knew that the tight budget meant poor materials would be used.

That reality was the jumping-off point for Cather's story of an engineer she named Bartley Alexander. His character represents the divided self. He is first seen as a happily married man, esteemed for his professional achievement. But during a stay in London, he meets Hilda Burgoyne, an Irish actress who had been his love a dozen years earlier, and they renew their love affair. The story becomes the ancient one of the eternal triangle, a person ruined by his failure to resolve the conflict in his character. In Cather's story, when the bridge collapses, Alexander is killed.

The public and reviewers liked *Alexander's Bridge*—but Cather did not. She began berating it as soon as it appeared, even telling friends not to bother reading it. It was a beginner's work, derived not from inner experience and pressure but from observation of the world outside. "Like most young writers, I thought a book should be made out of 'interesting material' and at that time I found the new more exciting than the familiar. The impressions I tried to communicate on paper were genuine, but they were very shallow."

Yet now at thirty-eight, she was no novice, for she had already published nearly forty short stories. If the novel was a bad start in her own view, perhaps it was, according to critic Louise Bogan, because Cather tried to write "beautiful prose about temperamental, ambitious, enchanting people." Bogan contends that Cather learned "her talents had no real scope in the drawing-rooms of New York and London."

In the spring of 1912, Cather traveled to the Southwest and visited her brother Douglass. He headed a construction gang for the Santa Fe Railroad in the little town of Winslow, Arizona. He had never married, and his sister found his rough life on the edge of the desert exciting. Eager to see more of the frontier, she wandered for months, dipping into New Mexico as well, enjoying contact with Native Americans and Mexicans, who reminded her of the beauty of ancient sculpture. Recovering her health, she rode, hiked, danced, and fell in love with the Southwest.

Her biggest discovery was of the ancient world of the cliff dwellers. She encountered it in Arizona's Walnut Canyon, where she saw the ruins of the multistoried cliff houses of Native American people. Archaeologists would find these had been built between the eleventh and the fourteenth centuries by Native Americans of the Anasazi culture. Their stone communal houses were placed on ledges in the canyon walls and on the the mesas

Cather (left) *and her brother Douglass* (right) *in Walnut Canyon, Arizona, in 1912*

(flat-topped rocks) for protection from nomadic predatory tribes. Below, in the river valleys, the Anasazi raised their crops.

Cather would return often to the Southwest—at least five times in the next fifteen years—using its history, traditions, culture, and people in her fiction. The stories she absorbed about Native American life and of the coming of the Spanish and the French missionaries would reach deep into Cather's emotional life and inspire the truth of her novels.

On her return from the Southwest, Cather made her temporary home once again at the McClungs in Pittsburgh. In her old attic room, she worked on "The Bohemian Girl," a story that had come to her when she stopped at Red Cloud. It is a tragic tale in which a Czech farmer surprises his wife who is with her lover, and he kills them both. That story finished, Cather looked at "Alexandra," the story she had written a year earlier. And suddenly she realized these two stories could combine into a novel. She called the new work *O Pioneers!*

The novel seemed almost to write itself. Cather had no skeleton framework in mind. Whatever happened in it was "spontaneous and took its own place, right or wrong. . . . This was the first time I walked off on my own feet—everything before was half real and half an imitation of writers whom I admired."

Cather took the criticisms of the "drawing room" setting of *Alexander's Bridge* to heart. In *O Pioneers!*—as in five other novels she would write—Cather chose to remember her Nebraska, when the railroad had opened up the prairie to her family and the

Cather began working on O Pioneers! as soon as she returned from her travels to the American Southwest. She is shown here in 1915.

other settlers she had come to know—Swedes, Norwegians, Germans, Czechs, and Russians. Not only was her setting totally familiar to her, but she presented several characters based on Nebraskans she had known. She wouldn't admit such identifications were real. No, each of her characters was a composite, quite consciously so, for she didn't want to hurt anyone's feelings. She would continue with this defense in the novels to come. But biographers have been able to pinpoint which among her family, neighbors, friends, teachers, and students were the models for the people on the printed page.

Those people, the immigrants she knew so well, were something new in American literature. What writer before her had treated them? Nebraska, too—the dry, flat, endless prairie—had never been the setting for a novel. When the *Philadelphia Record* reviewed *O Pioneers!* in 1913, the newspaper called it "a story of abundant merit" and added, "We hope Miss Cather will not neglect to till the promising field for fiction she is among the first to disclose."

Critics observed that the tone of the novel was nostalgic. An emotional quality of looking back with longing was typical of much of the writing to come. Cather was remembering the past and regretting that the present had lost the qualities she saw in the lives of people of bygone days.

It was from a poem by Walt Whitman that Cather took her title:

Have the elder races halted?
Do they droop and end their lesson, wearied
over there beyond the seas?
We take up the task eternal, and the burden
And the lesson,
Pioneers! O Pioneers!

She dedicated the novel to Sarah Orne Jewett.

CHAPTER NINE
A Passion for Music

THE REVIEWS OF *O PIONEERS!* would have delighted the author of any novel. "Magnificent . . ." "Far above the ordinary product of contemporary novelists . . ." "American in the best sense of the word . . ." "Touched with genius . . . ."

Almost at once letters poured in, inviting Cather to speak to women's groups or to writers' organizations. Elizabeth Sergeant said that Cather had no interest in putting herself on display. In fact, it angered the author. "When Willa talked of what she hated, her whole personality changed. Her chin hardened, her shoulders pushed forward, and one felt that the rigors of her life had made her rough or touchy. Her emotional nature was disciplined on the surface; but not far below burned a fiery furnace. When the wrong kind of person—for her—approached her with seeming kindness, an uncontrollable antagonism flashed out."

In 1912 Cather moved with Edith Lewis into a spacious apartment at 5 Bank Street in a quiet corner of Greenwich Village. The rent was forty-two dollars a month. They had several good-sized

85

rooms on the second floor of a brick, five-story house. The house was lit by gas, not electricity, and heated by coal grates. They needed more furniture, which they bought at auction, and had a carpenter build bookshelves. The floors were covered with their oriental rugs. Over the fireplace in the living room, Cather hung a large portrait of Baroness Dudevant, the French feminist and novelist who wrote under the pen name George Sand.

Settling in, they bought nothing more. "What money we had," said Lewis, "we preferred to spend on flowers, music, and entertaining our friends." Visitors enjoyed their Friday afternoon gatherings so much they would bring strangers along. "Everyone talked as if there were not nearly enough time for all they had to say. Often a small group of Willa's more intimate friends would stay on after the others had drifted away, lingering until eight o'clock or later, and the talk then was often at its best."

Rent was cheap in those long-ago days. And so were servants. They hired Josephine Bourda, recently arrived from France, to be their cook and housekeeper. No wonder there was little money to spare. To keep the fireplace going, Cather would tip the grocer's boy to go along with her to the docks where she'd buy a cartful of coal at a discounted price. Taxis? No, she used the bus or the trolley, or she walked.

S. S. McClure, no longer with the magazine he'd built, was hard up for money, deeply in debt. The new editors made him an offer. If he'd write the story of his extraordinary life, they'd publish it and apply the fee to money he owed a paper mill. That way, readers would think he was still part of the magazine.

The trouble was, McClure didn't write easily. He needed help. He wrote Cather, who was visiting New Mexico, to ask if she'd do it. She said yes without hesitation. In her reply (paraphrased by McClure's biographer, Peter Lyon, she did not allow her letters to be quoted directly), she said:

S. S. McClure asked Cather to help him write his memoirs.

Her heart was touched by his financial difficulties. She was alarmed and pained to hear of what had happened. She could not make herself believe that S.S., at his age, with such a career behind him, and with such specialized ability, could be kept down for long. She was sure that she could help out. She bade him count on her to do anything she could. She reminded him of how generous he had always been; it made her not only sad, she wrote, but mad, fighting Irish mad, to think that he was being so tormented and deviled about money. A few days later, back home in Red Cloud, Nebraska, she assured him that she would certainly help him write the autobiographical articles, nor would she ask for any pay for the work. She could do it better, she insisted, and would feel more zest in doing it, if there were no question of payment at all. He had done more favors for her than she could count; she wanted an opportunity to do him a small favor in return. . . . She was concerned only that perhaps she might not be able to write the articles just as he would like them; the events that sang one tune to him, she wrote, might sing another to her; the way in which one writes a thing, she reminded him, is not altogether under one's control. . . . Of her own affairs, she added that she had such a head-full of stories that she dreamed about them at night. She was so dark-skinned and good humored, after her weeks on horseback, that he would never know her. She begged him to forget how cranky she had got, when she had tired at the end of the long days in the office. Her holiday in the desert had taken all the kinks and crumples out of her; she felt as if her mind had been freshly washed and ironed.

She really loved this man and felt deeply obligated to him. But how would they work together? It was long before the era of tape recording.

They would meet, and he would talk to her, going into detail on the main events of his life, decisions, mistakes, and achievements. Cather listened, making no notes as he talked, for she did not want to break into his stream of consciousness. Then when he left, she would write down what he had said, trying her best to keep to his own language. What she added were links between episodes and, inevitably, a degree of her own perspective. The outcome of this collaboration was *My Autobiography*, by S. S. McClure. It ran in the magazine in series form from October 1913 to May 1914. And at year's end, it appeared in book form.

In 1913 *McClure's* asked Cather for an article on opera. Going to the opera became a regular delight for Cather. With her passion for music, she could not resist hearing the world's greatest singers performing at the Metropolitan Opera. Arturo Toscanini often conducted. She based her article on interviews with three great singers. One of them was the dazzling beauty, Olive Fremstad. Born of Swedish immigrants, she was raised in Minnesota. She was the most thrilling of all the opera stars, and Cather went to hear her nearly every time she sang. They quickly became friends, meeting often for tea or dinner, and the writer was invited to the singer's summer home in Maine.

That friendship led to Cather's next novel, *The Song of the Lark*. Its central figure is Thea Kronberg, an opera star, based in part upon Fremstad and in part upon herself. To Edith Lewis, who knew her so intimately, no character in Cather's novels "is more

Olive Fremstad was an opera singer with whom Cather became friends in 1913. Fremstad's career was the basis for Cather's novel The Song of the Lark.

purely imaginary than Thea Kronberg as a child and young girl. She is not taken from anyone Willa Cather knew. She is drawn partly from surmise as to what Olive Fremstad, the model for the latter part, might have been; partly, perhaps, from a composite of impressions about Scandinavians she had known. . . . But while the physical personality is entirely different, the person who most resembled the young Thea Kronberg in thought, in feeling, in spiritual development, is Willa Cather herself."

In her fiction to come, Cather's most frequent character model would continue to be herself. She believed that all artists—whatever the art they worked in—shared similar emotions, thoughts, moods, and skills.

Cather's work on *The Song of the Lark* was interrupted in 1914 by another serious illness. It began with a hatpin scratch on the back of her neck, beneath the hair. It became infected, causing pain so terrible she said it felt as if she had forty toothaches in the back of her head. She was sent to the hospital and, as the pain continued, begged the doctors for any and every painkilling drug. In treating her, they shaved off the hair on the back of her head. It made Cather feel as bad as if she had lost an arm or a leg.

Friends stood by her. Isabelle McClung came in from Pittsburgh, and Olive Fremstad brought in bouquet after bouquet of flowers. After three weeks of treatment, the hospital released Cather. But she had to see a doctor every day until all signs of the blood poisoning had gone. Had this occurred later, when antibiotics were available, she would have been quickly cured.

Depressed by her illness, Cather was unable to resume writing for a time. To lift her spirits, she tried to enrich the background for the novel. Vocal teachers let her observe lessons they gave, Fremstad got her into opera rehearsals, and she probed such offstage business as agents and contracts.

Then, suddenly, came the news that Fremstad, at forty-two, was retiring from the Metropolitan Opera. Cather and Lewis attended her farewell performance, in the role of Elsa in Wagner's opera *Lohengrin*. The audience gave her an unprecedented ovation that lasted a full forty minutes!

Hoping travel would speed recovery, Cather spent a couple of months with Isabelle McClung in Pittsburgh and then visited Fremstad in Maine. The soprano worked and played so hard that it exhausted Cather. Nevertheless, she went west in July, to Wyoming and Colorado, and by August was once again visiting family in Nebraska. That was when she heard the terrible news—war had started in Europe. World War I would soak the earth in blood.

CHAPTER TEN
A Hidden City—
A New Novel

THE NEWS OF WAR IN EUROPE jolted Americans out of their routine lives. Who could have predicted that the twentieth century would be a time of great wars that made the United States' war with Spain in 1898 look like a skirmish? Europe stumbled into World War I when a young Serbian terrorist murdered the Austrian archduke Franz Ferdinand at Sarajevo (now the capital of Bosnia and Herzegovina) on June 28, 1914. Ten million soldiers would die over the next four years.

News of the war's outbreak horrified Americans, but in Pittsburgh, at the McClungs', it seemed so remote. Cather was putting the finishing touches on *The Song of the Lark*. She worked at her usual rate: two to three hours each morning. She could produce no more—nothing like the French writer she so admired, George Sand. Legend held that Sand would finish a novel at three o'clock in the morning and begin another an hour later.

In the summer of 1915, Cather and Edith Lewis made their first trip together to the Southwest. Their destination was Mesa

Verde in the southwestern corner of Colorado. At the town of Mancos, they hired a team and driver for the 20-mile (32 km) ride to what had been a national park since 1906. The evening before they set out, Cather visited the elderly brother of Dick Wetherill, the young cowboy who had "discovered" the hidden city of Mesa Verde in 1888. He told Cather how his brother, while searching for lost cattle, had suddenly come upon an entire city of cliff dwellings, hidden for centuries. The homes had been carved into the caves of the porous rock. Why had Native Americans ceased to occupy their stone dwelling in the thirteenth century? It was a mystery no one had yet solved.

Cather (left, with unknown man) *and Edith Lewis* (right) *took their first trip west together in 1915. They would travel to the American Southwest together many times in the following years.*

Cather visited the Cliff Palace in Mesa Verde, Colorado, for the first time in 1915. First discovered in 1888, the Cliff Palace is the largest cliff dwelling in North America.

The two women stayed for a week, exploring Mesa Verde with the help of a forest ranger. They spent a whole day examining the Cliff Palace with its 223 rooms. Ten years later, Cather would describe the palace's giant tower in her novel *The Professor's House*.

After Mesa Verde, they visited Taos, a small town in New Mexico, not yet the artists' colony that would change it so much. They stayed at an adobe lodge run by a Mexican woman. On horseback they rode all over the countryside, meeting many Spanish-speaking villagers. Lewis felt how intensely attuned her friend was to these people and their land. Cather was storing memories she would use a dozen years later in *Death Comes for the Archbishop*.

She learned a great deal about the country and the Native Americans and their traditions from a farmer-priest, Father

Haltermann, whom she met in an old church at Santa Cruz, New Mexico. The longer she stayed in the Southwest, she recalled many years later,

> the more I felt that the story of the Catholic Church in that country was the most interesting of all its stories. The old mission churches, even those which were abandoned and in ruins, had a moving reality about them; the hand-carved beams and joists, the utterly unconventional frescoes [paintings on plaster walls], the countless fanciful figures of the saints, no two of them alike, seemed a direct expression of some very real and lively human feeling. They were all fresh, individual, first-hand. Almost every one of those many remote little adobe churches in the mountains or in the desert had something lovely that was its own. In lonely, sombre villages in the mountains the church decorations were sombre, the martyrdoms bloodier, the grief of the Virgin more agonized, the figure of Death more terrifying. In warm, gentle valleys everything about the churches was milder.
>
> During the twelve years that followed my first year in New Mexico and Arizona I went back as often as I could, and the story of the Church and the Spanish missionaries was always what most interested me; but I hadn't the most remote idea of trying to write about it. I was working on things of a different nature, and any story of the Church in the Southwest was certainly the business of some Catholic writer, and not mine at all.

Heading back east, Cather stopped at Red Cloud to visit her family, while Lewis went on to her job in New York. Apparently, Cather felt that always bringing a woman home with her might confirm a possible lesbian relationship and thus make the townsfolk uncomfortable. Edith Lewis would never accompany her to Red Cloud. But that didn't prevent any of the Cathers from visiting the two in New York.

After she left Red Cloud, Cather was not headed back to Bank Street. Instead, she wished to stay with Isabelle McClung for a time in Pittsburgh. But Judge McClung had just died and with her mother long gone, Isabelle told her friend she wished to sell the home. This was a shock to Cather, after so many years of enjoying that home. But worse news came. McClung announced she was going to be married. Her husband would be Jan Hambourg, a violinist who gave chamber music concerts in Europe and the United States. The impending marriage of her intimate friend of fifteen years was shattering news for Cather.

If not for this, Cather might have derived great pleasure from the publication of her novel, *The Song of the Lark*, in October. She had written much of it in Isabelle McClung's home, and the book was dedicated to her. It was a big book to heft: 490 pages in small type—three times as long as *O Pioneers!*

Cather felt that Fremstad, who had grown up in Minnesota, shared many of the traits Cather had cherished in her Nebraska neighbors. Although the new novel's setting is Colorado, in the first and longest part of the story, Cather is really writing about Red Cloud and her own family life.

So when Cather tells of her character Thea at the age of seventeen leaving for Chicago to study piano and finding that her real artistry is in singing, the reader will see Cather's experience when she entered the University at Lincoln. The twenty years Cather had reported on the arts and especially the music world of New York provides the groundwork for Thea's meteoric success as an opera star. Cather understood the complexities of artistic temperament and portrays them beautifully in Thea's character. She had learned too that while being a great artist may be thrilling, it comes at a price. As Thea says:

> Your work becomes your personal life. You are not much good until it does. It's like being woven into a big web. You can't pull

away, because all your little tendrils are woven into the picture. It takes you up, and uses you, and spins you out, and that is your life. Not much else can happen to you.

What would Olive Fremstad think of the novel that had been created out of her own life? Of course, she read it promptly. And loved it. She told Cather it was the only book about an artist she had read that dug deep down into the reality of that life.

CHAPTER ELEVEN
My Ántonia

IN APRIL 1916, Isabelle McClung married Jan Hambourg. His was a Russian Jewish family who had become British subjects and established homes in London, England, and Toronto, Canada. His father, Michael Hambourg, taught music and brought up his sons to be musicians: Jan, a violinist; Mark, a pianist; and Boris, a cellist. The trio had built a fine reputation for their chamber music concerts in Europe and the United States. The loss of her long intimacy with McClung was hard to bear, but what made it worse for Cather was her friend's choice of a Jew as her husband. There are traces of anti-Semitism in Cather's writings.

In the United States of those years, anti-Semitism was widespread. Huge numbers of immigrants were pouring into the country. Among the newcomers were hundreds of thousands of Jews from eastern Europe. They had fled violent persecution by the Russian czar (ruler). Did they belong?

In nonfiction pieces she wrote while working for *McClure's* and in the work of others she edited, there is blunt expression of

In 1916 Isabelle McClung (right) *married Jan Hambourg, a Russian-born violinist, who had a successful career as a soloist, chamber musician, and teacher.*

the paranoia many Americans felt about the danger of the large number of Jewish immigrants, which they termed an "invasion."

The scholar Lisa Marcus has pointed out those elements in Cather's fiction. In "The Diamond Mine," her portrayal of a Greek Jew, Miletus Poppas, is a nasty caricature. In "Scandal," she presents Siegmund Stein as an unscrupulous garment manufacturer. In still another story, "Behind the Singer Tower," a Jewish character, builder Stanley Merryweather, is accused of "unethical and stingy eagerness to cut corners despite risking workers' lives."

Later, in other works, Cather depicts likable characters drawn from Jewish neighbors she was fond of when living as a youngster in Red Cloud. Yet the reader may feel these are exceptions that prove the rule.

Soon after McClung's marriage, Cather and Edith Lewis returned to the Southwest for a long vacation. They stayed with Roscoe Cather's family in Wyoming, and then Cather sped on to Red Cloud when she learned her mother was ill. As the oldest child, Willa took over running the household, doing the cooking, and even making pastry they delighted in. She made sure to spend time with her childhood classmate Annie Pavelka on her farm and to see how her many children were coming along. Soon her neighbor would be transformed into the Ántonia of Cather's next novel.

She worked on the novel that winter and into the spring of 1917. Once she had decided that Pavelka would be the heart of her story, Cather had to devise a method for developing her. She could have had Pavelka tell her own story, but instead, she chose as her narrator the fictional Jim Burden—writing in the male voice again, despite Sarah Orne Jewett's advice. Still, Cather gave him many of her own attributes.

Later, on the sole occasion when Cather agreed to teach writing, at the Breadloaf Writers' Conference in Vermont, she was asked if there was a preconceived plot that novelists followed. She replied, "In *My Ántonia* there is no love story, no courtship, no marriage, no broken heart, no struggle for success. I knew I'd ruin my material if I put it in the usual fictional pattern. I just used it the way I thought absolutely true."

Much of the novel is based on the actualities of life on Nebraska farms and in the small town of Red Cloud. Individuals, families, major and minor characters, and crucial events can be pinned to the life Cather had known in her youth. Yet she was unaware of how rooted in actual experience some of the writing was. When her father read *My Ántonia*, he told his daughter that several of the incidents had come out of experiences she'd shared with him. It surprised her. She thought she had made them all up.

As the summer of 1917 came on, the Hambourgs, vacationing at an inn in Jaffrey, New Hampshire, urged Cather to join them. She took rooms at the inn and liked that part of New England so much she would spend many future autumns in Jaffrey. During those weeks she spent with Isabelle and her husband, Cather said she came to like him. But her tone when she spoke reminded people of the way some say, "Oh, that man's not so bad when you get to know him." Alfred Knopf, who would later become her publisher and close friend, believed Cather never lost her prejudice against Jan Hambourg.

While in Jaffrey in 1918, the proofs of *My Ántonia* came in from Houghton Mifflin and Cather read them, with Lewis helping. Lewis described Cather's approach to editing her own work:

> After a thing was written she had an extremely impersonal attitude toward it. If there was "too much" of anything, she was not only ready, she was eager to cut it. She did not cherish her words or phrases. Sometimes she would have a sudden illumination and would make some radical change—always I think, for the better.

One of her biographers, James Woodress, holds that *My Ántonia"* is probably one of Willa Cather's greatest works. In it theme, character, myth and incident ride together comfortably on a clear, supple prose style. Everything went right—a splendid concept executed with perfect taste and mastery. . . . The wonder of it all is that the novel, so rich in suggestiveness, is so artfully simple."

One of the leading critics of that time, H. L. Mencken, wrote that "*My Ántonia* is not only the best novel done by Miss Cather, but also one of the best any American has ever done."

This illustration by W. T. Benda from Cather's novel My Ántonia *features immigrants waiting on a sidewalk.*

Despite such a review, sales were not large at first. For it was an unconventional novel. It lacked the form readers were used to. Cather provided no tightly woven plot and no grand hero. Her focus was on "ordinary" farm folk. Reading the novel many years later, Justice Oliver Wendell Holmes wrote that "It is a poem made from nature . . . that being read establishes itself as true, and makes the reader love his country more." And the poet Louise Bogan called it "an undoubted American masterpiece which will be read when most contemporary novels are as outdated as the publishers' blurbs on their jackets." They were right. Gradually, Cather's novel won readers who have kept the book in print ever since.

When the *New York Times* interviewed Cather several years after *My Ántonia* was published, the reporter asked, was it a good book "because it is the story of the soil"? And Cather answered, "No, no, decidedly no. It was the story of people I knew. I expressed a mood, the core of which was like a folksong. . . . That it was powerfully tied to the soil had nothing to do with it. But I might have written the tale of a Czech baker in Chicago, and it would have been the same. It would have been smearier, jollier, noisier, less sugar and more sand, but still a story that had as its purpose the desire to express the quality of these people."

CHAPTER TWELVE
One of Ours: A Pulitzer Prize

DURING THE TIME THAT CATHER had been waiting for *My Ántonia* to reach the public, she went back to Red Cloud for a visit. In May 1918, her young nephew, Grosvenor Cather, whom she had known from his childhood, had been killed leading his men into combat in France. His mother let Willa read her son's letters home. He had volunteered and in his letters expressed how happy he was to be in the service. (He had been miserable in Nebraska.)

Another soldier Cather had encountered was David Hochstein, a young violinist. She had met him at a concert in New York and was taken by his personality and his musicianship. She saw him again after the United States entered the war in 1917 and found him in doubt about the war's aims and what he should do. In the end, he volunteered and wrote back how much he loved the companionship he had found. He too was killed—on November 10, 1918, the day before the armistice was declared.

Cather wrote One of Ours *about her cousin, Grosvenor Cather, who died fighting in World War I.*

Their letters suggested the different ways a man could change under the extreme pressure of war. They led Cather to plan a novel about the nature of such men and the meaning of their lives. It was a formidable task she was taking on—dealing with men and with bloody combat she had never experienced. It would take her more than three years to complete the novel, which she would call *One of Ours*.

World War I was a war out of which would come notable novels by young Americans who had served in it: *Three Soldiers,* by John Dos Passos; *A Farewell to Arms*, by Ernest Hemingway; and *The Enormous Room*, by e. e. cummings. What could she accomplish, so remote from the scene, the soldiers, and the action? She protested that hers was not a war novel. That was not its true focus.

While working on the story at Bank Street, she met many young soldiers through one of her former high school students, now stationed at an army post in New York. They would talk with Cather for hours about their military experience.

She went up to Jaffrey to continue work on the novel in the autumn of 1918. There she met a doctor who had served as a medical officer on a troopship (a ship for carrying troops) where a flu epidemic broke out. He let Cather make use of the diary he'd kept during that bad time.

Then, in the spring of 1920, a critical change occurred in Cather's literary life. By this time, *My Ántonia* had been out for eighteen months. But sales were so slow her income was worrisome. She hadn't liked Houghton Mifflin's design of her novel, yet her complaints went unheeded. She had noticed books coming from a new company, Alfred A. Knopf. Knopf and his wife, Blanche, seemed utterly devoted to high quality and to books and authors for their own sake. Cather decided to barge in to their office and see what would come of it.

Though without an appointment, she was welcomed by young Alfred Knopf, and a long conversation began. He "seemed to have more degrees and shades of color in both his likings and his scorn than most people have," Cather recalled. "And he seemed to be going into this business as if it were an exhilarating sport of some kind. His talk was amazingly free and human."

The meeting ended with Cather asking if Knopf would become her publisher. He replied that they'd both better think it over. It was a serious matter. At their second meeting soon after,

Left to right: *Alfred Knopf, his son Alfred, and wife, Blanche, aboard the* S.S. Carinthia *in the 1920s*

Knopf said he'd try it out if she had something ready. She was in the middle of the war novel and could suggest only a batch of her short stories. He agreed to take those, and a few months later, Knopf published *Youth and the Bright Medusa*.

The new book contained four stories from the earlier collection, *The Troll Garden*, and four others not collected before. Among these were "The Diamond Mine" and "Scandal." Knopf would remain Cather's publisher for the rest of her life.

Cather visited France in 1920 to tour the battlefields of World War I. Here she stands in front of a tent in Cavaliere, France. Cather toured the battlefields with Jan and Isabelle Hambourg.

Cather and Isabelle Hambourg at Ville–d'Avray in France. Someone wrote their names on the photograph.

With her stories safely in Knopf's hands, Cather sailed with Lewis to Europe. The final section of her novel would take place in wartime France. The battlefields were still raw, and she wanted to see them before finishing her writing. They stayed for two months in Paris, visiting the famous Louvre museum and going to the opera. Isabelle and Jan Hambourg arrived in Paris and took Cather on a two-week tour of the devastated battlefields of northeast France.

When *Youth and the Bright Medusa* came out upon her return, it received good reviews. One praised it for her portraits of "the quality of ambition in women," who sometimes became the victims of great success. Another critic spoke of her remarkable ability to get under the skin of her characters. And Phyllis C.

Robinson, a biographer, suggested that "Willa's own mood may be judged by the common theme that links the tales, the passion of the artist to create and the thwarting of his desire by a hostile and mercenary society."

The writing of the novel, *One of Ours*, went very slowly during 1920 and into 1921. The setting at the beginning is Cather's Nebraska. The central character is Claude Wheeler (based on her nephew). He has two brothers, Bayliss, a successful businessman, and Ralph, a whiz with any kind of machinery. David Gerhardt in the novel is the violinist David Hochstein. Claude himself is a young farmer who falls into a loveless marriage with Enid Royce, a tireless campaigner for the prohibition of alcohol.

The coming of the war in Europe changes Claude's dismal life. What happens to him in the army gives him a sense of the youthful joyousness he had missed out on. He experiences the splendid friendships with men like David Gerhardt that can develop in times of war.

But by the time Cather neared the end of her writing, she had lost all hope that the war might open a new era, changing the world for the better. In the last pages of *One of Ours*, her soldiers are seen to have died for nothing.

The reviews were mixed. Some critics who had admired her earlier work were disappointed. Cather didn't know what she was talking about, said one critic: "She should stick to her farms."

Heywood Broun, an old admirer, wrote angrily that Cather's hero "loses his life and finds his soul. We happen to believe that there is such a thing as setting too high a price even upon souls and war is too high a price." Much later, James Woodress would write that while the novel is not carelessly written, "seldom does it rise above the level of competent journeyman work." But other critics welcomed the novel with high praise, calling it her most powerful work and the peak achievement of this literary artist.

The controversy may have contributed to the novel's success. It was Cather's first best seller, and it stimulated sales for *My Ántonia* as well. In 1923 *One of Ours* won the coveted Pulitzer Prize for the most distinguished fictional work of the year by an American author.

From this point on, Cather's literary reputation was established. New books would sell well and old books would remain in print. Schools and colleges would place her work in their curricula. She would never again have to worry about money. She and Edith Lewis would live well wherever they liked, travel anywhere, and see plays and operas whenever they chose. Cather would continue her generosity with family and neighbors back in Red Cloud, helping farmers meet mortgage payments during the Great Depression (1929–1942) and always sending gifts at Christmastime.

Cather writes while leaning on a wooden half wall in Jaffrey, New Hampshire, in the mid-1920s.

CHAPTER THIRTEEN
When the World Broke in Two

WITH *ONE OF OURS*, Cather reached a turning point in her life. She was forty-nine when the novel appeared. Many years later, looking back on that time, she said, "The world broke in two in 1922." It was not because she had lost the desire to write. In the ten years after *One of Ours*, she would publish seven more novels. But her spirits fell and her health deteriorated during this time. Did she feel disheartened because the life she had known in her childhood on the prairie had changed so much? She has her character Claude Wheeler say that his young generation of farmers were "either stingy and grasping, or extravagant and lazy."

Negative reviews of *One of Ours* were more upsetting than usual, for that novel, she said, "took more out of me than any book I ever wrote." Following its publication, she continued to suffer periods of poor health, including neuritis [nerve injury] in her right arm and shoulder and three serious attacks of influenza.

During the summer of 1922, Cather and Lewis looked for a new retreat from the heat and noise of the big city. They rented a

Left: *Cather holds a walking stick as she poses at her property on Grand Manan, New Brunswick, Canada. Cather built a cottage there* (below).

small cottage on Grand Manan, a wooded island in Canada's Bay of Fundy. The cottage was more than a hundred years old, had no plumbing, and the rickety walls invited drafts on every side. Cliffs hundreds of feet high bordered the island. The ever-changing weather was enchanting. Wildflowers grew everywhere, and wild animals roamed the woods. The two women could cherish solitude without loneliness for there was abundant life on the water—fishing crews on boats of many kinds, lumberjacks, and Indians out for work or for fun. They liked the climate too—warm, bright days; cool nights; and even the spells of rainy weather. Cather thought it the best place she had ever found for writing. (Two years later, she had a cottage built there, overlooking the cliffs and the sea.)

Cather set to work on *A Lost Lady*, a new novel she had struggled with for some time. At the heart of the story is Mrs. Marian Forrester. She is a direct portrait of Mrs. Silas Garber, the young second wife of the aging man who had founded Red Cloud and served two terms as Nebraska's governor. (Both Garbers were now dead.) In her adolescent years, Cather had been fond of Mrs. Garber.

The novel depicts the feverish desire to get rich quick, and the pain and loss it causes others. Characters Cather once celebrated as pioneers are now condemned for the ruthless theft of land that the Native Americans had lived on for centuries. The characters in the novel proved to be so recognizable in Red Cloud that some people grew angry and even threatened lawsuits. Cather said it never occurred to her to write the story until the actual model for Mrs. Forrester had died, and there were no children who could be hurt.

During that summer of writing it, however, Cather rewrote chapter after chapter, changing point of view, cutting, and adding. Her sense that the world had broken in two after the war is felt not only in this novel but in the two that followed. Her characters believe that contemporary life has deteriorated badly. It leads them to reexamine the past. Was it so good? So promising? Or did they fail to recognize how bad it really was?

As 1922 wound down, Cather went to Red Cloud for Thanksgiving and to celebrate her parents' fiftieth wedding anniversary. In December, Cather and her parents were confirmed in the Episcopal Church. Though raised as a Baptist, she found the ritual of her new community an affirmation of an ancient religious spirit she cherished.

In the 1920s, Cather was interviewed by many newspapers. In one of these, the book columnist Burton Rascoe described her as "full-blooded, vigorous, substantial, sure of herself, matter-of-fact, businesslike, and somehow I had expected her to be reticent, uncommunicative, rather sweet and softish. She looks as though

Cather (back, third from left) *on one of her many visits to Red Cloud to visit her family. Also pictured are her parents, Jennie* (second from left) *and Charles* (fifth from left), *and sister Jessica Cather Auld* (sixth from left) *and her family.*

she might conduct a great law practice or a successful dairy farm, superintend a telephone exchange or run a magazine with equal efficiency, ideas and energy."

Taking Cather to lunch, he noted her fondness for food. She told one friend that she had studied cooking under the guidance of Josephine Bourda, the French cook who had worked for her for fifteen years. She did better as a student in that course than in all the others she'd taken. Trouble was, now if she wanted to eat something really good, she had to go into the kitchen and make it herself. At a gathering of gourmets in London, those present agreed that Willa Cather was "one of the two best women cooks in the world." (Who was the other one? Emma Goldman, the Lithuanian-born anarchist.)

Cather photographed in the mid-1920s

Describing her looks, Rascoe said, "Her features are bluntly decisive in line; her eyes are pale blue and set wide apart, with eyebrows high enough to give her ordinarily a look of challenge and appraisal; her mouth is ample, with full, flexible lips whose movements are as expressive an accompaniment of her speech as are the gestures of a Latin; and her nose is a nose, not a tracery." As for how she dressed, a local reporter said that "she breezed into Cleveland Friday morning in a bright green and gray fur coat with gold and black velvet toque [hat], and bright green bag to match."

When *A Lost Lady* was published in 1923, the short novel was called by the *New York Times* "simply a little work of art." The

Nation said that while not a great novel, it was almost a perfect one. Heywood Broun, who had attacked *One of Ours*, welcomed this new novel as "truly a great book."

When the novel sold well, Warner Bros. reportedly paid ten thousand dollars for the movie rights. The film premiered in Red Cloud. The audience liked it, and they believed it captured the Garbers. But Cather thought it was false. She would never again allow her novels to be turned into movies or plays. And in her will, she repeated that strict command.

In the summer of 1923, the idea for her next novel, *The Professor's House*, came to Cather during a stay in Paris. She saw an exhibition of old and modern paintings by Dutch artists while visiting the Louvre. In some paintings of heavily furnished interiors, "there was a square window, open, through which one saw the masts of ships or a stretch of gray sea. The feelings of the sea one got through those square windows was remarkable, and gave me a sense of the fleets of Dutch ships that ply quietly on all the waters of the globe."

How would she attain the feeling of freedom from the material world that she felt by looking through those painted windows? Through a novel about Godfrey St. Peter, his family, and his favorite student—Tom Outland, a brilliant young engineer. Tom, engaged to Rosamond, the professor's daughter, is killed in the war. Rosamond marries another man, Louie Marcellus, and they are rapidly enriched by her inheritance of Tom's invention, an airplane engine.

The peaceful pattern of the professor's family is torn apart by the changes wealth brings to everyone's life. The professor, aged fifty-two—Cather's age as she wrote the novel—teaches at a midwestern university. Over the years, he has seen the quality of both the students and the faculty decline. They are not interested in the humanities but in making lots of money as fast as possible. The campus comes to feel more like a trade school than a university.

Willa Cather (sitting) *and artist Leon Bakst in his studio in Paris, France, in October 1923. A portrait of Cather was commissioned that year, and Cather chose Bakst to do the painting. The portrait hangs in the Omaha Public Library in Omaha, Nebraska.*

At the same time, the professor is troubled by the sense that he is on the verge of moving from middle age into old age.

With those Dutch paintings in mind, Cather tried to make the first part of the novel feel overcrowded and stifling with new things that money leads to—houses, furniture, clothing, petty ambition, and quivering jealousies—until the reader feels stifled.

Then, in the next part, she would open that square window and let in the fresh air. And for this, she goes back in time about twenty years to tell of Tom's life before entering the university. With lyric simplicity, she presents the first-person story of how Tom discovers the village of cliff dwellers in the New Mexico canyon. The contrast between the petty lives of the people of wealth in the college town and the dignity and beauty of the centuries-gone community provides the reader with a shift of emotion and mood. That part of the novel was created out of Cather's own experience at Mesa Verde years before.

Edith Lewis held that this novel represented Cather's increasing concern as an artist—"The bringing into being of something beyond the situation or the characters of a story, something beyond the story itself—the unseen vision, the unheard echo, which attend all experience."

In the last part of the novel, the professor, alone while his family is in Europe, narrowly escapes death from a gas leak. When he recovers, he realizes he is no longer the same man. It is a change he accepts quietly—one that his family will never be aware of.

CHAPTER FOURTEEN
Peace—and Serenity

THE PROFESSOR'S HOUSE earned favorable reviews and sold well. *Collier's* magazine bought the serial rights for ten thousand dollars. Cather then went out and bought herself a mink coat, the kind of luxury she'd never indulged in before. She was being showered with honorary degrees at major universities, including her own University of Nebraska.

Her next novel, *My Mortal Enemy*, was written in the early months of 1925. Scarcely eighty pages long, it tells the story of Myra Henshawe, a young woman who turned away from wealth to marry for love. Romantics would think that choice would assure happiness. But no, Myra is made to suffer for it.

The story leaps ahead ten years. Myra tries to make her friends believe her marriage is still a romantic dream. But she has quietly betrayed friendships and suspects her husband has betrayed her by having affairs with other women. Living in poverty, she returns to the Catholicism of her youth, which promised an enduring relationship her own life has missed.

Right: *Ever since her late college years, Cather kept up with the latest fashions. Here she wears a mink coat that she purchased in 1924.*

Left: *Cather wrote an inscription in this copy of* My Mortal Enemy *in 1931. It says: "This story is rather a favorite of mine, and I hope you will like having it from me, on the eve of my departure."*

As she is dying, Myra murmurs, "Why must I die like this, alone with my mortal enemy?" The novel can be seen as Cather's views on love vs. material pursuits.

The critics' response to the short novel was mixed. It sold well, however, partly because it raised a debate over who the "mortal enemy" was. Myra's husband? Or Myra herself?

From *A Lost Lady* to *The Professor's House* to *My Mortal Enemy*, there is an unrelenting trend downward into bitterness in Cather's work. But in her next novel, her mood changes to one of optimism.

She began intense work on *Death Comes for the Archbishop* in the summer of 1925 and in six months had completed it. The novel came out of her many visits to the Southwest over a period of fifteen years.

On one of her visits to the Southwest, Cather met Father Haltermann and saw the good work he had done. She learned, too, of some of his predecessors and of the priest she calls in her book Father Jean Marie Latour.

The novel's setting is New Mexico of the 1850s. This is soon after the United States' war with Mexico, which ended with the incorporation of about one-third of Mexico's land—California, Arizona, Nevada, Colorado, Utah, and New Mexico—as territories of the United States. That war was the product of expansionist forces carefully engineered by President James K. Polk.

The prologue to the book is her response to a painting by the French artist Jehan Georges Vibert that she had seen in the Louvre. Called *The Missionary's Return*, it showed a pioneer priest, his garments dull and worn, but his face all alight, telling a group of richly robed cardinals of the hardships and glories of missionary work in some far part of the world.

In front of the cathedral in Santa Fe, Cather had seen the bronze statue of Archbishop Jean Lamy, a French pioneer priest. And in a book by Father William J. Howlett about the life of Father Joseph P. Machebeuf, she had learned a great deal about his work in close relationship with Archbishop Lamy. Lamy, she said, had become "a sort of invisible personal friend."

The scholar Marilee Lindemann suggests that the two priests Latour and Vaillant whose great love infuses the novel are a rare turn for Cather's fiction, where so often intimacy leads to disaster. In the novel, the two priests grew up in neighboring parishes in France, but did not meet until attending seminary. They decided to go abroad together as missionaries. They work together productively and when they are separated for long intervals, feel it deeply. Their utopian aim in New Mexico is to cleanse the church of any errors or wrongdoing and thus hold it safe.

The two priests are not unaware of what power, wrongfully used, can do to people under its domination. Near the end of the novel, Bishop Latour says, "I have lived to see two great wrongs righted; I have seen the end of black slavery and I have seen the Navajos restored to their own country." He wonders if there will ever be an end to wars with the Indians. And Cather adds, "Too many traders and manufacturers made a rich profit out of that warfare, a political machine and immense capital were employed to keep it going."

The novel moves along, incident after incident portraying the priests, Mexicans, Indians, the rich, the poor, and even Kit Carson, the legendary frontiersman. Cather meant to avoid the typical plot, building to a grand climax. Instead, she treats each human experience, whether big or little, as of equal significance, in a spiritual sense.

After Father Vaillant departs on a mission to Colorado, Bishop Latour calmly waits for death, convinced that death will be a means of someday reuniting him with his beloved friend.

Cather's biographer James Woodress believed this novel "gave her the peace she had been seeking and the serenity to face her last two decades."

CHAPTER FIFTEEN
The Great Depression

CATHER WAS FIFTY-FOUR when *Death Comes for the Archbishop* was published in 1927. Writing that book, she told a friend, was the greatest pleasure of her life. In telling the story of the archbishop, she felt she was living right alongside him.

She was now at the peak of her career. Her novels were being translated into several languages. They sold very well, and critics hailed her as one of the United States' best. But that same year, she was forced to leave her beloved Bank Street home. The subway system needed that space, and the building was torn down. She and Edith Lewis moved to the Grosvenor, an apartment hotel at 35 Fifth Avenue.

In December Cather began a long vacation back home in Red Cloud. With her father, she revisited the old immigrant communities and caught up with lives she'd written into her stories. She returned to New York in late February. And only a week later, she rushed back to Red Cloud because her father had suffered a sudden heart attack. He died the day before she arrived.

Willa Cather's parents, Jennie and Charles Cather, in the mid-1920s

Friends had died before, but this was the first loss within her family. She had loved her father dearly and found his going hard to take. The loving fathers in her fiction are patterned on Charles Cather. His death meant it would be the end of that home, for her brother Douglass, who did not wish to leave their mother alone, took her back with him to California.

The year 1928 never got any better. Cather and Lewis went up to Grand Manan. Mourning for her father, Cather tried to ease the pain by writing and produced three short stories, reviving her childhood years in Red Cloud. In one of these, "Old Mrs. Harris," she re-creates her family—her young mother and father, her grandmother, and the next-door neighbors, the Wieners. In 1932 Knopf would publish the three in one volume called *Obscure Destinies*.

Returning to New York in the fall, after a brief stop in Quebec, Canada, Cather learned her mother had suffered a paralytic stroke in California from which she would never fully recover.

The brief stopover in French Catholic Quebec would lead to Cather's next book—*Shadows on the Rock*. Writing it would take a long time. She would make four more research trips to Quebec and another trip to France to secure the historical background needed for this novel.

Cather in 1925

Shadows on the Rock is set in Quebec, in the Canada of the seventeenth century. French settlers pioneering in Canada established Quebec City in 1608. While visiting France, Cather had found in the Louvre the diary of an apothecary [pharmacist] who had worked in Quebec. The apothecary's diary was so fascinating, Cather filled notebooks with its rich details and from that and other sources was able to bring that time and place alive. As she had often done before—building characters on family, friends, and neighbors—this time she relied on neighbors of French ancestry in Jaffrey, New Hampshire.

The book is the story of how the townsfolk live through the changing of the seasons. The main character is the apothecary Auclair, a widower with a young daughter, Cecile, who will marry a dashing young woodsman. Several other characters are linked in friendship with them. The theme is the value of a stable existence in contrast with an ever-changing society. The apothecary believes he is so lucky "to spend his old age here where nothing changed."

Asked what that novel was about, Cather answered:

An orderly little French household that went on trying to live decently, just as ants began to rebuild when you kick their house down, interests me more than Indian raids or the wild life in the forests. . . . And really, a new society begins with the salad dressing more than with the destruction of Indian villages. Those people brought a kind of French culture there and somehow kept it alive on that rock.

She is telling readers she's not interested in the big events but rather in how a culture is shaped. Something like the way an anthropologist examines a society.

To accomplish her writing goals, Cather needed to protect her privacy. It was hard to do when she was expected to appear at universities to accept all those honorary degrees. In 1928 alone, she refused twenty-four invitations to speak on programs or serve on various boards. In 1929 came perhaps the highest honor—election to the National Academy of Arts and Letters. That only multiplied requests from the press for more interviews.

Once, caught by a reporter as she was about to board a train, she was asked what she considered to be the greatest obstacle American writers had to overcome. She replied, "It's the lecture bug . . . very dangerous for writers. We get a little more owlish and self-satisfied all the time. We hate it at first . . . but in the end we fall in love with the sound of our own voice. There is something insidious about it, destructive to one's finer feelings. Try it out yourself . . . and you'll see how puffed up and important you begin to feel."

Cather went out to California more than once to offer what comfort she could to her mother, whose life was fading. Working on her novel helped sustain her when back in the East. Her mother died in 1931, just as the new novel was published. *Shadows*, like *Archbishop*, climbed high on the best-seller list and soon became her most popular novel. Both books are historical novels. The earlier one moves forward over many years, while the new novel takes place within just one year.

When *Shadows on the Rock* appeared, the Great Depression was already in its second year. The sudden collapse of the U.S. economy in October 1929 signaled the beginning of a period of widespread global unemployment and poverty. Many millions of Americans suffered anguish and desperation that Willa Cather was fortunate to escape. The sale of books decreased sharply for several years. Some publishing houses went bankrupt. Several magazines stopped buying stories or quit publishing altogether.

In the early years of the Great Depression, a number of young writers made the economic crisis and its devastating effect upon workers and middle-class people the focus of their stories and novels.

Willa Cather was luckier. Nearing sixty, her talent over the years had produced an assured income, enabling her to avoid the

John Steinbeck on Writers in the Depression

John Steinbeck, unknown at the time, but later to become a Nobel Prize winner for his novels, was living in California in the early 1930s. Living free in an old cottage by the shore, he gathered from the sea food to eat and driftwood to keep warm. He was part of a group of young people, all poor and living the same way. Of that hard time, he said, "We pooled our troubles, our money when we had some. Only illness frightened us. You had to have money to be sick—or did then. Being without a job I went on writing." His work went out and just as regularly came back. No sale. "Publishers were hardest hit of all. Given the sea and the gardens, we did pretty well with a minimum of theft. We didn't have to steal much. Keeping clean was a problem because soap cost money."

shock younger writers experienced. She would write two more novels during the 1930s, but neither touched on the misery of that decade.

Critics and reviewers were angered by Cather's seeming indifference to the tragedy of the Great Depression. They wanted and they expected writers of her quality to deal with its grim realities. She was a romantic, some said, focused exclusively on the dim past, unwilling or unable to grapple with a changed world.

That view of Cather's work would change, with time.

CHAPTER SIXTEEN
A Circle of Friends

WHEN *OBSCURE DESTINIES*, a volume of short stories, was published in 1932, Cather and Edith Lewis moved out of the Grosvenor Hotel, as Cather had never liked it. She thought of finding a house in the country or maybe even moving to San Francisco, California. But when Lewis said she wanted to keep her job in the city, they rented a spacious apartment at 570 Park Avenue and moved in toward the end of the year.

Cather's move to one of the city's most affluent neighborhoods came just as Franklin Delano Roosevelt was elected president. He acted swiftly to obtain from Congress broad executive powers to wage war against the economic emergency. Federal relief came first and then billions to provide public works so the unemployed—including writers, artists, actors, and musicians—could find jobs. Roosevelt's New Deal government provided a public agency, the Federal Writers Project, to sustain those in need while they continued to write. Some of the best talents the United States has known were in the project: Saul Bellow, Richard Wright,

Nelson Algren, John Cheever, and Ralph Ellison. They were paid $23.86 a week and were expected to put in thirty hours and produce between 1,200 and 2,000 words a week. That left writers time and energy to do their own creative work, if they wished.

With the decline in energy that so often comes with aging, Cather withdrew from contacts with the world outside. She was so little in touch with the nation's suffering that she criticized government action to provide welfare. She thought civil servants were dreary, petty people whose only pleasure lay in frustrating imaginative, daring people.

What she missed was the great change taking place in the national temper. As President Roosevelt put it: "Today there is a real and forceful belief on the part of the great mass of the people

Cather stands outside her cottage on Grand Manan Island in the early 1930s.

that honest, intelligent and courageous government can solve many problems which the average individual cannot face alone in a world where there are no longer one hundred and twenty acres of good free land for everybody."

That "good free land" the president referred to included Cather's own Nebraska. Its southern region was part of the Dust Bowl of the 1930s. The dust storms of that era ranked among the worst environmental disasters in world history. Three hundred million tons (272 metric tons) of soil were blown away during dust storms that went on for seven long years. And that disaster came on top of a ten-year depression among farmers who had already mortgaged their land to the hilt by the time the Great Depression began in 1929. The farmers of Cather's Nebraska were among the militant thousands who grabbed pitchforks and monkey wrenches and demonstrated against prices so low that crops were being sold for less than cost.

Cather did respond to cries for help when they rose from people she knew. When she heard her old boss, S. S. McClure, had fallen on hard times, she joined a few of her former workmates to provide him (anonymously) with a regular monthly sum of money.

When she learned how badly off her Nebraska friends were, she sent them food, clothes, and a stream of checks. She felt guilty to be vacationing on cool Grand Manan Island while friends were burning in Dust Bowl heat.

Cather had always liked to have young people around her. And beginning in 1930, she became the center of a small circle of wonderful new friends. They were the musical Menuhin family. The parents were Russian Jews—Moshe and Marutha, and the children, at the time Cather met them, were Yehudi, fourteen; Hepzibah, ten; and Yalta, nine. She had met the family through the Hambourgs when visiting them in Paris in 1930.

Her friendship with the Menuhins was one of the greatest

Cather befriended the Menuhin family in 1930, including siblings (left to right) *Hepzibah, Yehudi, and Yaltah.*

pleasures that came to her in later years, said Edith Lewis. Yehudi, an extraordinary prodigy, began playing the violin at the age of four. His career included concerts given around the world. His sisters were prodigies too: Hepzibah, a violinist; and Yaltah, a pianist. They appeared in recitals with their brother and on the international concert circuit.

The youthful energy of the Menuhin brood recharged Cather's energy. She had been a regular at the Metropolitan Opera for many years, and now she added symphony concerts and chamber music to her must-see list. Knopf gave her a fine record player, and Yehudi added a gift of all his recordings. Much later, as adults, the Menuhins heard others say that Cather had been sorely depressed in those years. But the children never saw any sign of it. Yalta told her son that her own character was molded by Aunt Willa, as they called her. And Yalta's work to become a musician was inspired by the teaching of that same mentor.

Perhaps the best picture of Cather's intimate ties to those children is found in a memoir by Edith Lewis, who saw day by day what she describes:

> I remember the Menuhin family's winter visits to New York, as sort of continuous festival, full of concerts and gay parties; orange trees and great baskets of flowers for Willa Cather arriving in the midst of snow-storms; birthday luncheons, with Russian caviar and champagne; excursions to the opera, where she took Yaltah and Hephzibah to hear *Parsifal* for the first time; long walks around the reservoir in Central Park, when the three children all wanted to walk beside her, and had to take turnabout. They discussed very abstract subjects together—art, religion, philosophy, life. . . .
>
> She had a feeling that Hephzibah and Yaltah, traveling in so many countries, and learning something of the language of each, were never going to get a thorough sense of the English language; and this worried her. She asked Marutha Menuhin if she might organize a Shakespeare Club, with no one allowed to be present except herself and the little girls. Yehudi then asked if he might come too.
>
> They began with *Richard II*, and went on to *Macbeth* and *Henry IV*. Willa Cather hunted through the bookstores of New York to get each of the children a copy of these plays in the original Temple Edition, the only one she herself cared to read; it was then rapidly going out of print.
>
> She was greatly touched when, many years afterward, Yehudi told her he had found and bought a complete second-hand set of the Temple *Shakespeare*, in a shop in New Orleans.

It was now that Cather would begin to work on a new novel, *Lucy Gayheart*, whose characters would include musicians. But nothing like the Menuhins.

CHAPTER SEVENTEEN
Virginia: Beginning and Ending

CATHER'S NEXT NOVEL BEGINS in Nebraska, in a small town like Red Cloud, and then moves on to Chicago, where Lucy Gayheart, a young pianist, has a love affair with a middle-age and married concert singer. She has left behind a young lover whom she rejected and who feels he can never forgive her. Cather had known a young Red Cloud woman like Lucy, whose memory had teased her mind until, perhaps influenced by her friendship with the Menuhins, she constructed a story with musicians once again at its core. It is a tragic tale with two deaths—whether accidental or suicidal, the reader must decide.

As she was finishing her draft of the novel, handwritten as was her custom, Cather sprained the tendon of her right wrist. Inflammation set in and became so painful she couldn't hold a pencil or type a word. Treatment helped for a while, but the inflammation returned, now to both wrists. An orthopedist made a brace that left her fingers free. Still, she could barely write a few words. She was forced to dictate letters. But dictating her stories?

135

That, for her, was impossible. She had always written the first drafts by hand, not on a typewriter like most authors of her time. She dreaded the years ahead. How would she manage? Living in pain day after day?

That affliction, Edith Lewis noted, "made the simplest acts of life, which ordinarily one performs unconsciously—taking a bath, dressing oneself, tying a knot, opening a letter—wearisomely difficult and irksome. Willa Cather rarely let it depress her spirits, or affect her independence. I remember her telling once, when some one offered to help her, how, when she was a very little child, and her parents would try to assist her in something, she would protest passionately: 'Self-alone, self-alone!'"

When *Lucy Gayheart* appeared in 1935, the reviews were disappointing, although the book became a best seller. Cather admitted to friends that her interest in writing it had fallen off. She could not create in Lucy the intensity needed because she did not feel it herself. But she never wrote sloppily, and reviewers agreed there are many fine passages in the novel that are characteristic of the earlier Cather.

After *Lucy Gayheart*, three years passed before Cather took on another novel. Her beloved friend Isabelle Hambourg fell sick with what proved to be a terminal illness. In the hope of finding a cure, she and her husband Jan came to the United States. While Jan gave concerts, Cather stayed at Isabelle's hospital bedside day after day. When the doctors gave permission for Isabelle to join her husband in Chicago, Cather accompanied her there and then visited them in Europe for what turned out to be the last time.

During 1935 Cather edited a collection of her essays to be published the next year as *Not under Forty*. All but one of the pieces had appeared earlier. She cut and revised to improve them. Her mood that year can be seen in the book's title. She wants the reader to know she's well over forty (she was sixty-three in 1936), and her book is meant for old-timers.

Cather on her sixty-third birthday in 1936

When younger critics in the 1930s accused her of being a romantic who refused to recognize life as it is, she replied she was opposed to artists using their creative power to reform society. That was propaganda, not literature.

Cather wrote one story during 1935 and spent most of the next year on preparing a library edition of all her works. She took little pleasure in that heavy task. She cut, transposed, and rearranged her works to please herself, viewing them anew from this distance in time. At least doing the work herself gave her complete control of how her writing would be read in the future. To make sure that would still be true when she was gone, she insisted none of her letters be published or her works be anthologized after her death. No one but the artist who created a work should have the right to modify or adapt it in any way, she believed.

Such complete editions were sold by subscription, not through bookstores, and Knopf did not do that. Her old publisher, Houghton Mifflin, worked out an arrangement with Knopf to handle the set. *The Novels and Stories of Willa Cather* was published in twelve volumes, and later, when Cather's final novel appeared, it was added to the set.

That fall of 1937, with great difficulty, Cather began work on what would be her last novel, *Sapphira and the Slave Girl*. She would not complete it until three years later. And that seems a marvel considering the grievous loss of so many of her family and friends in that time. Her brother Douglass died of a heart attack in June 1938. Cather couldn't believe that as the oldest of seven children, she would outlive any of the others. She was so stricken by the news that she couldn't attend his funeral.

Then, four months later, came the dreaded news that Isabelle Hambourg had died. Cather had been too weak and weary to visit her in that last year. When Jan Hambourg returned to Cather all her letters to his wife, she had them burned. She grieved for months, unable to carry on her writing. She had written her stories especially for her beloved Isabelle. But there were countless others who felt she had written for them—readers everywhere. And their letters thanking her for what she had done for them kept pouring in.

In the spring of 1938, Cather and Lewis traveled to Cather's Virginia birthplace, to renew her memories of the people and scenes that figure in *Sapphira and the Slave Girl*. She had never placed a novel there. Perhaps it was memories stirred by the death of her parents that led her to write it now. The book was difficult for her to write. Her first draft was two or three times as long as the final one.

By the time the novel was published in 1940, World War II (1939–1945) had started. And France, the country she loved, had surrendered to Germany. On the day of that surrender, Cather noted in her diary, "There seems to be no future at all for people of my generation."

The novel begins in the Shenandoah Valley of Virginia in the decade before the U.S. Civil War. A plantation family and their slaves are central to the action. Sapphira Colbert is the ill and aging owner of the slaves, married to a man who detests slavery but continues to live with it. The central action is the decision of their daughter Rachel to help the young slave Nancy escape to freedom in Canada on the Underground Railroad. In an epilogue set twenty five years later—when Cather herself as a little child witnesses the action—Nancy returns from Canada as the free and independent woman she has become.

Sapphira is not depicted as a heroine. She is a tyrannical, cold, repellent figure. And her husband, though a decent, tender, well-intentioned man, is shown to lack the will to act on his convictions.

The scholar Ann Romines held that part of Cather's inheritance was the bland memory of slavery created by white southern historians in the late nineteenth and early twentieth centuries. Theirs was an idealized view of the plantation as "Sweet Home." It glorified "the faithful black slave, especially the mammy, and sought to con-

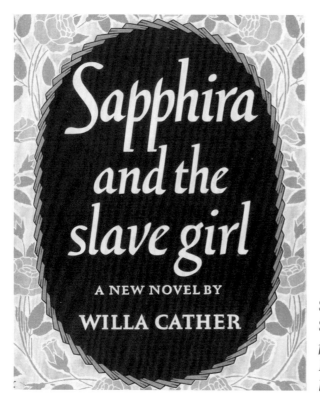

Sapphira and the
Slave Girl *was
published in 1940.
It would be Cather's
last novel.*

ceal alternative memories of violence, exploitation and cruelty."

Knopf speeded publication of *Sapphira* so that it would appear on December 7, 1940, the day of Cather's sixty-seventh birthday. The reviews were favorable, some holding it to be her finest work, although the work did provoke controversy. Critics differed on the interpretation of the characters and the story, and on where her sympathies lay.

By 1940 the damage to Cather's hand had become so severe that she had to be hospitalized for weeks. She and Lewis went west that summer for a happy monthlong reunion in San Francisco with her brother Roscoe and his wife. On the way, they passed through the Southwest for what would be a last look at the region she had used so creatively.

On the way home, they traveled across Canada. On December 7, 1941, Cather's sixty-eighth birthday, the Japanese attacked Pearl Harbor, Hawaii, bringing the United States into the war. For much of 1942, Cather continued to be ill, with a gallbladder operation adding to her troubles. Yet, according to Lewis, she never allowed her weakening condition to damage her real self. "To any occasion that moved her strongly, she would rise with full command both of the situation and herself, with all her natural force and ardour."

In the few years remaining, Cather and Lewis summered at Northeast Harbor in Maine rather than travel to Grand Manan. They rented a small cottage belonging to the nearby Asticou Inn. Cather spent endless hours reading the novels of Sir Walter Scott, a pleasure she had not sought when young.

Cather had the germ of an idea for another novel in mind, one to be set in Avignon, France. But the condition of her hand was so crippling that she failed to get very far in the story. During those summers, she did succeed in creating two short fictions. One of these, "The Best Years," she wrote for her brother Roscoe, in memory of their life together as children. In 1945, just as she completed it and was about to send it to him, word came that Roscoe had died in his sleep.

These were the war years, with deaths occurring everywhere and on so massive a scale as to seem impossible. Cather's letters express her deep concern for the men and women among her family and friends who were serving in the military.

The world they had known was crumbling, laid to waste by bullets and bombs. Cather felt so despairing at times that she wondered why the most brilliant scientists had devoted their genius to wartime means of destruction. Not science and technology, she believed, but art and religion were humanity's only hope for happiness.

In her last years, she knew moments of joy in visits from a niece, a letter from a childhood friend, the recorded music of Mozart, and the poetry of Chaucer and Shakespeare.

WILLA CATHER
December, 1876—

THE TRUTH AND CHARITY OF HER GREAT
SPIRIT WILL LIVE ON IN THE WORK
WHICH IS HER ENDURING GIFT TO HER
COUNTRY AND ALL ITS PEOPLE

...that is happiness, to be dissolved
into something complete and great

From My Ántonia

Cather is buried in Jaffrey, New Hampshire.

On the last day of Cather's life, April 24, 1947, Edith Lewis said, "Her spirit was as fresh, her grasp of reality as firm as always. And she had that warmth of heart, that youthful fiery generosity which life so often burns out."

Willa Cather died suddenly that afternoon of a cerebral hemorrhage. Four days later, she was buried on the site she had chosen, a hillside in Jaffrey, New Hampshire.

Chronology of Willa Cather

1873   Wilella Cather is born December 7 in Back Creek Valley, near Winchester, Virginia, the first of seven children.

1883   The Cathers move to Webster County, Nebraska.

1884   Her father quits farming, moves the family to Red Cloud, and opens a real estate and loan office.

1890   Willa graduates from Red Cloud High School. She enters the University of Nebraska at Lincoln.

1891   Her essay on Thomas Carlyle appears in two publications.

1892   Her first short story is published.

1893   She begins writing for the *Nebraska State Journal*. Drama reviews establish her reputation.

1895   She graduates from the university. Cather begins part-time newspaper work for the *Lincoln Courier* and writes short stories.

1896   She moves to Pittsburgh, Pennsylvania, to edit *Home Monthly*, a family magazine. Cather contributes also to the *Pittsburgh Daily Leader*.

1897   *Home Monthly* is sold, and she loses her job. She takes an editing job with the *Pittsburgh Leader*.

1898	The Spanish-American War is fought.
1900	She resigns from the *Daily Leader*.
1901	Cather lives with Isabelle McClung and her family. She begins her teaching career, first at Central High School and then at Allegheny High School.
1902	With Isabelle McClung, Cather makes her first trip to Europe.
1903	*April Twilights*, a volume of poetry, is published. Her short story appears in *Scribner's*. Cather meets S. S. McClure, editor and publisher of *McClure's Magazine*, who likes her writing. She meets Edith Lewis, a Lincoln native, on a visit home.
1905	*The Troll Garden*, a collection of short stories, is published. She spends the summer in the West with Isabelle McClung.
1906	Cather joins *McClure's Magazine* and moves to New York City. She moves in with Edith Lewis, a coworker at *McClure's*.
1907–1908	Cather moves to Boston on assignment from *McClure's*. She meets Sarah Orne Jewett and Annie Fields. Cather is promoted to managing editor of *McClure's*. She goes abroad with Isabelle McClung.
1911	Cather leaves *McClure's*. She completes her first novel, *Alexander's Bridge*.
1912	*Alexander's Bridge* is published. She visits her brother Douglass in Arizona and travels in the Southwest. Cather begins writing *O Pioneers!* With Edith Lewis, she rents an apartment at 5 Bank Street, their home for the next fifteen years.

1913	*O Pioneers!* is published. She ghostwrites McClure's *My Autobiography* to run serially in his magazine and appear in book form a year later.
1914	World War I starts in Europe.
1915	She learns Isabelle McClung is to marry Jan Hambourg. *The Song of the Lark* is published.
1917	The United States enters World War I. Cather receives an honorary degree from the University of Nebraska. She writes *My Ántonia*.
1918	Her nephew is killed in the war. She plans *One of Ours*, a novel about World War I. *My Ántonia* is published.
1920	Cather travels to Europe with Edith Lewis. Knopf, Cather's new publisher, releases *Youth and the Bright Medusa*, a collection of short stories.
1922	*One of Ours* is published.
1923	She wins the Pulitzer Prize for *One of Ours*. *A Lost Lady* is published.
1925	*The Professor's House* is published. Cather has a cottage built on Grand Manan, an island in Canada.
1926	*My Mortal Enemy* is published.
1927	*Death Comes for the Archbishop* is published. Cather and Lewis move to Grosvenor Hotel, New York.
1928	Cather's father dies. Her mother has a paralytic stroke. Cather visits Quebec.
1929	She is elected to the National Academy of Arts and Letters. She receives an honorary degree from Yale. The Great Depression begins.

1930　She visits her mother in California. Cather visits France. She receives a Gold Medal of the American Academy of Arts and Letters for *Death Comes for the Archbishop*. Cather meets the Menuhin family.

1931　Cather is given an honorary degree from Princeton. Her mother dies. *Shadows on the Rock* is published.

1932　*Obscure Destinies*, a book of short stories, is published. Cather moves to 570 Park Avenue with Edith Lewis.

1933　Cather receives an honorary degree from Smith College. She develops a chronic inflammatory wrist and hand injuries that hamper her writing.

1935　*Lucy Gayheart* is published.

1936　*Not under Forty*, a collection of essays, is published.

1937　She prepares a library edition of *The Novels and Stories of Willa Cather*.

1938　Her brother Douglass dies. Isabel McClung Hambourg dies.

1939　World War II starts.

1940　*Sapphira and the Slave Girl* is published on Cather's sixty-seventh birthday. She visits her brother Roscoe in California.

1941　Japanese attack Pearl Harbor. United States enters World War II.

1944　Cather receives a Gold Medal from the National Academy of Arts and Letters.

1945　Her brother Roscoe dies. World War II ends.

1947　Cather dies at home in New York on April 24. She is buried in Jaffrey, New Hampshire.

1948　A collection of short fiction, *The Old Beauty and Others*, is published posthumously.

Source Notes

9 Mildred R. Bennett, *The World of Willa Cather* (Lincoln: University of Nebraska Press, 1951), 93.

15 James L. Woodress, *Willa Cather: Her Life and Art* (New York: Pegasus, 1970), 55.

15 Ibid., 38.

21 Janis P. Stout, *Willa Cather: The Writer and Her World* (Charlottesville: University Press of Virginia, 2000), 10.

22 E. K. Brown and Leon Edel, *Willa Cather: A Critical Biography* (Lincoln: University of Nebraska Press, 1953), 25.

25 Bennett, 170.

26 Ibid., 44.

28 Willa Cather, *My Ántonia* (New York: New American Library, 1994), 138.

28 Bennett, 170.

32 Woodress, 48.

37 Ibid., 55.

40–41 L. Brent Bohlke, ed., *Willa Cather in Person* (Lincoln: University of Nebraska Press, 1986), 181.

41 Milton Meltzer, *Milestones to American Liberty* (New York: Thomas Y. Crowell, 1961), 160.

50 Bohlke, 2.

50 Edith Lewis, *Willa Cather Living: A Personal Record* (Lincoln: University of Nebraska Press, 2000), 47.

52–53 Bohlke, 2.

54 Woodress, 91.

54 Ibid.

56 Ibid., 93.

56 Stout, 89.

57 C. Douglas Sterner, "A Splendid Little War," July 11, 2007, http://www .homeofheroes.com/wallofho nor/spanish_am/01_intro .html (October 12, 2007).

62 Woodress, 101.

62 Bohlke, 179.

63–64 Lewis, xxvii.

65 Stout, 89.

69 Phyllis C. Robinson, *Willa: The Life of Willa Cather* (New York: Holt, Rinehart & Winston, 1983), 148.

69 Ibid.

70 Willa Cather, *Willa Cather on Writing* (Lincoln: University of Nebraska Press, 1988), 50.

71 Ibid, 51.

71 Ibid, 54.

71 Ibid., 102.

72 Alice Booth, "Willa Cather Who Believes There Is Nothing in the World Finer to Write about Than Life, Just as It Is, and People, Just as They Are," *Good Housekeeping* (September 1931), 196–198.

76 Woodress, 130.

77 Lewis, 66.

81 Woodress, 143.

81 Bohlke, 115.

83 Woodress, 156.

84 Bohlke, 7.

84 Walt Whitman, *Whitman Poetry and Prose* (New York: The Library of America, 1982), 371.

85 Brown and Edel, 181.

85 Edith Shepley Sergeant, *Willa Cather: A Memoir* (Lincoln: University of Nebraska Press, 1953), 117.

86 Bennett, 182.

87–88 Peter Lyon, *Success Story: The Life and Times of S.S. McClure* (New York: Charles Scribner's Sons, 1963), 342.

89–90 Lewis, 39.

95 Cather, *Willa Cather*, 5.

96–97 Willa Cather, *The Song of the Lark* (Boston: Mariner Books, 1983), 392.

99 Merilee Lindemann, ed., *The Cambridge Companion to Willa Cather* (New York: Cambridge University Press, 2005), 75.

100 Bohlke, 77.

101 Lewis, 106.

101 Woodress, 179.

101 Lewis, 108.

102 Woodress, 183.

102 Bohlke, 114.

103 Ibid., 172.

106 Lewis, 110.

110 Robinson, 219.

110 Ibid., 228.

110 Woodress, 192

110 Stout, 83

112 Woodress, 196.

112 Willa Cather, *One of Ours* (New York: Barnes and Noble, 1992), 92.

112 Woodress, 197.

114–115 Bohlke, 63.

115 Ibid., 65.

116 Ibid., 86.

116 Ibid., 88.

116 Ibid.

117 Robinson, 239.

117 Bohlke, 192.

119 Lewis, 138.

122 Willa Cather, *My Mortal Enemy* (New York: Vintage Press, 1990), 85.

123 Robinson, 247.

123 Willa Cather, *Death Comes for the Archbishop* (New York: Knopf, 1927), 290.

123 Woodress, 225.

127 Ibid., 235.

127 Lindemann, 58.

128 Bohlke, 90.

129 Milton Meltzer, *Brother, Can You Spare a Dime? The Great Depression: 1929–1933* (New York: Facts on File, 1991), 52.

131–132 Ibid., 117.

134 Lewis, 170.

136 Ibid., 175

139 Ibid., 184.

139–140 Lindemann, 220.

141 Lewis, 192.

142 Ibid., 196.

Selected Bibliography

Acocella, Joan. *Willa Cather and the Politics of Criticism*. New York: Vintage, 2000.

Ambrose, James. *Willa Cather: Writing at the Frontier*. New York: Oxford University Press, 1988.

Bennett, Mildred R. *The World of Willa Cather*. Lincoln: University of Nebraska Press, 1951.

Booth, Alice. "Willa Cather Who Believes There Is Nothing in the World Finer to Write about Than Life, Just as It Is, and People, Just as They Are." *Good Housekeeping*, September 1931, 196–198.

Brown, E. K., and Leon Edel. *Willa Cather: A Critical Biography*. Lincoln: University of Nebraska Press, 1953.

Cather, Willa. *My Mortal Enemy*. New York: Vintage Press, 1990.

———. *One of Ours*. New York: Barnes and Noble, 1992.

———. *The Song of the Lark*. Boston: Mariner Books, 1983.

———. *Willa Cather on Writing*. Lincoln: University of Nebraska Press, 1988.

Lee, Hermion. *Willa Cather: Double Lives*. New York: Pantheon Books, 1989.

Lewis, Edith. *Willa Cather Living: A Personal Record*. Lincoln: University of Nebraska Press, 2000.

Lindemann, Marilee. *Willa Cather: Queering America*. New York: Columbia University Press, 1999.

———, ed. *The Cambridge Companion to Willa Cather*. New York: Cambridge University Press, 2005.

Lyon, Peter. *Success Story: The Life and Times of S.S. McClure*. New York: Charles Scribner's Sons, 1963.

Meltzer, Milton. *Brother, Can You Spare a Dime? The Great Depression: 1929–1933*. New York: Facts on File, 1991.

O'Brien, Sharon. *Willa Cather: The Emerging Voice*. New York: Oxford University Press, 1987.

———, ed. *New Essays on* My Ántonia. New York: Cambridge University Press, 1999.

Reynolds, Guy. *Willa Cather in Context: Progress, Race Empire*. New York: St. Martin's Press, 1996.

Robinson, Phyllis C. *Willa: The Life of Willa Cather*. New York: Holt, Rinehart & Winston, 1983.

Rolfe, Lionel. *The Uncommon Friendship of Yalta Menuhin and Willa Cather*. Los Angeles: American Legends Publishing, 2004.

Rosowski, Susan. *The Voyage Perilous: Willa Cather's Romanticism*. Lincoln: University of Nebraska Press, 1986.

Sergeant, Elizabeth Shepley. *Willa Cather: A Memoir*. Lincoln: University of Nebraska Press, 1953.

Skaggs, Merrill Maguire. *After the World Broke in Two: The Later Novels of Willa Cather*. Charlottesville: University Press of Virginia, 1990.

Skaggs, Merrill Maguire, ed. *Willa Cather's New York: New Essays on Cather in the City*. Madison, NJ: Fairleigh Dickinson University Press, 2000.

Stout, Janis P. *Willa Cather: The Writer and Her World*. Charlottesville: University Press of Virginia, 2000.

Urgo, Joseph R. *Willa Cather and the Myth of American Migration*. Urbana: University of Illinois Press, 1995.

Woodress, James L. *Willa Cather: A Literary Life*. Lincoln: University of Nebraska Press, 1987.

———. *Willa Cather: Her Life and Art*. New York: Pegasus, 1970.

Reading Willa Cather Herself

WORKS OF WILLA CATHER

Original editions are cited here. A great many editions of Cather's writings have been published and are available in libraries, schools, and bookstores. In the instances where editions other than the original are cited in the text, the reprint edition appears in the bibliography.

NOVELS

Alexander's Bridge. Boston: Houghton Mifflin, 1912.

O Pioneers! Boston: Houghton Mifflin, 1913.

The Song of the Lark. Boston: Houghton Mifflin, 1915.

My Ántonia. Boston: Houghton Mifflin, 1918. Revised, 1926.

One of Ours. New York: Knopf, 1922.

A Lost Lady. New York: Knopf, 1923.

The Professor's House. New York: Knopf, 1925.

My Mortal Enemy. New York: Knopf, 1926.

Death Comes for the Archbishop. New York: Knopf, 1927.

Shadows on the Rock. New York: Knopf, 1931.

Lucy Gayheart. New York: Knopf, 1935.

Sapphira and the Slave Girl. New York: Knopf, 1940.

SHORT FICTION

The Troll Garden. New York: McClure, Phillips & Co., 1905.

Youth and the Bright Medusa. New York: Knopf, 1920.

Obscure Destinies. New York: Knopf, 1932.

The Old Beauty and Others. New York: Knopf, 1948.

Willa Cather's Collected Short Fiction, 1892–1912. Edited by Virginia Faulkner. Introduction by Mildred Bennett. Lincoln: University of Nebraska Press, 1965. Revised, 1970.

Uncle Valentine and Other Stories: Willa Cather's Uncollected Short Fiction, 1915–1929. Edited by Bernice Slote. Lincoln: University of Nebraska Press, 1972.

POETRY

April Twilights. Boston: Richard G. Badger, 1903.

April Twilights and Other Poems. New York: Knopf, 1923.

COLLECTIONS

The Kingdom of Art: Willa Cather's First Principles and Critical Statements. Edited by Bernice Slote. Lincoln: University of Nebraska Press, 1967.

Not under Forty. New York: Knopf, 1936.

Willa Cather in Person: Interviews, Speeches, and Letters. Edited by L. Brent Bohlke. Lincoln: University of Nebraska Press, 1986.

Willa Cather on Writing: Critical Studies on Writing as an Art. New York: Knopf, 1949.

The World and the Parish: Willa Cather's Articles and Reviews, 1893–1902. 2 vols. Edited by William M. Curtin. Lincoln: University of Nebraska Press, 1970.

Writings from Willa Cather's Campus Years. Edited by James R. Shively. Lincoln: University of Nebraska Press, 1950.

Internet Resources

Cather Foundation
http://www.willacather.org
Dedicated to preserving and promoting understanding and appreciation of the life, time, settings, and work of Pulitzer Prize-winning author Willa Cather, the foundation offers tours of historic Willa Cather sites in and around Red Cloud. There's also an extensive list of links to other Cather-related websites.

The Willa Cather Archive
http://cather.unl.edu/
The University of Nebraska's Willa Cather Archive contains Cather's writings, letters, interviews, and speeches, as well as biographical information and a large selection of photos.

Willa Cather Bibliography Database
http://www.willacatherbib.org/
A comprehensive Cather bibliographic database that is searchable by keywords, titles, authors, and dates.

Willa Cather State Historic Site
http://www.nebraskahistory.org/sites/cather/
The Nebraska State Historical Society operates the Willa Cather State Historic Site. Its museums and archives hold a large amount of information on Cather and late nineteenth-century Nebraska history.

Index

About the Author

Milton Meltzer has written more than one hundred books for young people and adults. The life of Willa Cather is the latest in his series of biographies of major American writers. Others include Henry David Thoreau, Walt Whitman, Edgar Allan Poe, Herman Melville, Nathaniel Hawthorne, Emily Dickinson, Mark Twain, and Langston Hughes.

Meltzer is the recipient of two awards honoring him for his lifetime body of work: the American Library Association's Laura Ingalls Wilder award and the Catholic Library Association's Regina Medal. Five of his books have been finalists for the National Book Award. He has won the Carter G. Woodson, Christopher, Jane Addams, Jefferson Cup, Olive Branch, and Golden Kite awards. His titles frequently appear on the Best Books of the Year lists of the American Library Association, the National Council for the Social Studies, the National Council of Teachers of English, and the *New York Times*.

Meltzer and his wife, Hildy, live in New York City. He is a member of the Authors Guild, American PEN, and the Organization of American Historians.